YOU ARE MY GOD

By the same author

My God is Real
One in the Spirit
Live a New Life
I Believe in Evangelism
I Believe in the Church
Is Anyone There?
How to Find God
How to Win the War
Called & Committed
Grow & Flourish

DAVID WATSON

YOU ARE MY GOD

**A Pioneer of Renewal
Recounts His Pilgrimage in Faith**

Harold Shaw Publishers
Wheaton, Illinois

Library of Congress Cataloging in Publication Data

Watson, David C. K., 1933-1984
    You are my God.

    1. Watson, David C. K., 1933-1984.   2. Church of England—Clergy—Biography.   3. Anglican Communion—England—Clergy—Biography.
4. Pentecostalism—Church of England—History—20th century.   5. Church renewal—Church of England—History—20th century.   6. Church of England—Doctrines.   7. Anglican Communion—Doctrines.   I. Title.
BX 5199.W376A38   1984   283'.3 [B]   84-1311
ISBN 0-87788-972-4

94   93   92   91   90   89   88   87   86   85   84
10   9   8   7   6   5   4   3   2   1

To all my Christian brothers and sisters in York who shared with us, both in joy and in pain, through the seventeen best years of our life.

Contents

Introduction

For years I have resisted pressure from others to write about our experiences leading the church in York. The growth of a congregation from almost nothing to 700 or more can be overrated. Many other churches have moving stories to tell, and besides, both at St. Cuthbert's and St. Michael-le-Belfrey in York, our own congregation had suffered in the past from too much exposure. Added to that, I knew that the apparent triumphalism of Christian "success" stories could sometimes discourage those who were battling with ordinary problems. I was also acutely aware of the spiritual dangers of the "cult of personality." This phenomenon is interesting to observe in the secular sphere of superstars, but it is divisive in the Christian church. Cults of personality caused problems at Corinth in New Testament days, and, sadly, they do the same in some Christian circles today.

The Christian gospel is not about superstars: "so let no one boast of men" wrote the apostle Paul (1 Cor. 3:21). The gospel is about God's extraordinary grace in spite of very ordinary human faults and failings, and about his blessings in the midst of sufferings. With these truths in mind I have tried to write honestly about both the pains and the joys—in my personal spiritual pilgrimage, in our corporate experiences as a congregation in York, and in Anne's and my marriage. Both Anne and I know that the Christian church has no immunity from the marriage problems that afflict society so widely today. For this reason we agreed that I should be deliberately open in writing about the difficulties that we too have experienced, especially now that we have worked through these traumas to a more mature and strong relationship.

The glib message of "Come to Christ and all will be well!" or "Be filled with the Spirit and your problems will be solved!" finds no echo in the pages of the New Testament. Certainly God promises us the "unsearchable riches of Christ," and the epistles are full of superlatives: love which surpasses knowledge, peace which passes all understanding, unutterable joy. But interwoven with these are the darker threads of pain and tears, weakness and sin, suffering and strife. The astonishing Good News of Christ is that he loves us just as we are and can work through us just as we are. No human frailty need hinder God's infinite grace.

Obviously I have had to choose selectively and carefully from a wide range of material, and the book may be more remarkable for what it does not say than for what it does. Where possible I have tried to avoid painful references to any individuals since these would not help anyone. My ultimate purpose is to give a personal testimony to the reality of God in the varied spectrum of human experience. If through the sunshine and storms something of the light of Christ is seen in greater glory, the book will not be in vain.

I wish to acknowledge the help of many people in the writing of *You Are My God.* I am especially grateful to Anne, my wife, for her wise advice as I wrote the manuscript and for her patient acceptance of me over the years, without which this book could never have been written.

I have valued too the encouragements and suggestions of a number of friends who read the manuscript, in particular Teddy and Margaret Saunders, Michael and Sylvia Mary Alison, Rob Warner, and Edward England, my literary agent, whose shrewd counsel I constantly treasure.

Most of all I want to thank Hilary Saunders, my secretary, both for her helpful comments during the exacting time of writing and for her untiring efforts with the typewriter.

1

An Experiment
of Faith

"I'LL SEE YOU THERE AT FOUR," said Sam, reflecting my cynical grin, as we accepted yet another invitation.

Our little scheme was working well. As long-time school friends, Sam and I had just started at Cambridge University. Like all other first-year students we were bombarded with invitations to join every conceivable activity from tennis to tiddlywinks, fencing to philosophy. All the clubs were offering sherry parties or teas to entice us into membership. So Sam and I decided to go to every event but join nothing. We listened patiently to Marxists waxing eloquent about the struggle of the masses, Tories extolling the virtues of free enterprise, oarsmen talking tantalizingly about steaks for breakfast, and Scotsmen explaining how to breathe some Highland sanity in the midst of mad dogs and Englishmen. We even went to the Christian Union at four o'clock one day. No group was too bizarre for us.

Like Sam, I was a cynical unbeliever—a humanist I called myself. My religious background was somewhat complicated. I had been brought up as a Christian Scientist since my father, a classical scholar studying at Oxford, adopted that faith at the start of World War One. For many intellectuals in those days it was the fashionable thing to do, for the intriguing concept of the power of mind over matter had captured the inventive imagination of many forceful personalities.

To be honest, almost the only thing I remember about Christian Science as a child was my Sunday School teacher telling our group of six- and seven-year-olds that if we had enough faith we could throw ourselves over a cliff and we would float down as safely as if held up by a parachute. This is not typical of Christian Science teaching, but to this day it is all that I can remember being taught. Fortunately I never experimented since I had no faith in my faith.

My other memory was that my father never allowed a doctor near our home, believing as he did that there is no reality in any sickness, rather it's all a matter of the mind. When my father, an active officer with the Royal Artillery, was away for many months at a time, my mother, a nominal Anglican, would surreptitiously ask a doctor to come when I had mumps or measles, but such medical interference would have been strongly disapproved of by my father. So firm were his beliefs that when he was suffering in India from acute bronchial pneumonia, he refused all medical assistance—and died. The disease which supposedly had no reality killed him. The power of the human mind was an insufficient savior.

I was ten at the time, and it was 1943. My gentle, newly-bereaved mother did the wisest thing she knew (for which I am now profoundly grateful). She had me quickly "done" in the Anglican church: I was baptized and confirmed, becoming a server in our parish church. Perhaps our local priest had never prepared a Christian Scientist for confirmation before, but I did not understand a word of what he said, and I found the sung eucharist every Sunday a ghastly and meaningless ritual which I assumed must be good for my soul since it made me so miserable.

Inevitably I suppose, I began to look in other directions for God, or at least for some kind of spiritual reality. I took part in a few seances, curious to know if I could get in touch with my father. The experience left me not only disillusioned but with a healthy awareness that I had been dabbling in something dangerous. I now realize that every involvement with the occult—spiritualism, astrology, tarot cards, witchcraft and all the "black arts," even horoscopes—is like playing with an unexploded bomb. You never know when it may go off. I have counseled numerous people who have been harmed in one way or another, some of them seriously, through occult experiences. It is literally a devilish business.

During my teenage years I tried a labyrinth of religious paths: theosophy, the anthropomorphism of Rudolf Steiner (my uncle was a devotee of his), and various forms of Buddhism. I was generally intrigued by the mysticism of eastern religions and once wrote a paper arguing strenuously for reincarnation since I found in this belief the only logical solution to the universal question as to the purpose of suffering. But God was nowhere to be found—he was the Great Unreality in my life.

My school days were mostly enjoyable and I was satisfactorily successful, but all religious instruction was a total non-event from my point of view. Just once or twice I thought I glimpsed a fleeting shaft of spiritual light breaking through the dense fog of confusion. I was intrigued by a Franciscan monk who gave a series of Lenten addresses at school. We all said, "Wasn't his talk tremendous!" to give the impression that, of course, we understood every word; but, like most of my friends I am sure, I failed to grasp anything at all with clarity. His brown "dressing-gown" and open-toed sandals fascinated me, though I wondered how on earth anyone with any intelligence could go around like that for the sake of Christ. In fact, every contact with the church reinforced my growing conviction—"It's not for me!" The real straw came during my two years in the Army.

In many ways they were marvelous years. Naturally there were a few less-than-positive moments, such as when I sank my troop of self-propelled guns in a stinking bog on the first day of massive military maneuvers. I had surveyed the ground fairly quickly, so as to position four guns, giving covering fire for the infantry. The ground seemed somewhat swampy, but in all other respects it was an excellent gun position. The guns swept in without too much difficulty; but when they "tracked" to respond to different angles of fire, each gun crew reported in turn that they were beginning to sink. We had to pull out and find another position, which, had it been a real battle, would have been unpardonable. As we pulled out, we discovered that the ground on which the guns had been standing was the firmest in the whole area. Moving forward they plunged into a sea of thick, black bog. The verbal response I received from my supervisors almost burnt out our radio communication system. Never before or since have I seen tanks become submarines within a few seconds: it was immensely impressive, and I doubt if any other junior officer has accomplished the same feat with such skill.

But for most of my time in the Army I made a lot of friends, played a variety of sports and went to countless parties, including some eye-opening shockers in the red-light district of Hamburg, Germany, called the Reeperbahn, which was notorious for its nightclubs, brothels, and strip-tease shows. After one of the worst of these evenings, we were chased through the streets of Hamburg at about 4 A.M. The German police cars had a tough time stopping our pepped-up Mercedes, but we eventually gave in to about twelve of them. It was the nearest to a James Bond chase scene that I have ever been in, and only our lack of sophisticated 007 equipment caused us to lose. It seemed to be a breathtaking adventure; in reality it was a sordid, stupid, drunken dare which exposed the emptiness of our hearts—a vacuum that cried out to be filled.

Army-style religion, however, couldn't fill that inner void in my heart. Technically an Anglican, I went to the regimental services—every decent officer was expected to do so—but the only active Christian I remember meeting was the padre, who seemed to be by far the heaviest drinker in our regiment. Ten years later I discovered that during the time I was in the army our padre had been suffering a severe nervous breakdown. Ignorant of that, I took his behavior as my final proof of the futility of the Christian faith, and I became an atheist. Over the years I had found no spiritual reality, and I easily convinced myself that I was philosophically on target in saying "There is no God!"

I can remember only one real prayer, if you can call it that, which I prayed during those years. After an especially wild party, while lying on my bed still dressed in my dinner jacket and suffering a splitting hangover, I said aloud, "O God, there must be a better life somewhere!"

Not by any stretch of the imagination did I expect such a drunken heart-cry to be answered in the way God chose. It was that four o'clock tea organized by the Christian Union at Cambridge University. Had I asked his opinion, my freshman cohort Sam would have said that I made two fatal mistakes that afternoon: I wore my old school tie, and I caught the speaker's eye on my way out.

After nondescript refreshments organized by undergraduates who all seemed to me to have bright eyes, perpetual smiles, and silly lapel buttons, we all had to sit down and listen to a young Anglican clergyman. I paid little attention to his words, since I did not believe in God anyway, but I heard him stress that the heart of the Christian faith was a personal relationship with Jesus Christ. I could not recall anyone ever having told me such a thing before, and I had to admit, reluctantly, that there was something unusually gracious and appealing about this clergyman. Unlike most other religious people I had so far met, he seemed to speak from genuine personal experience, with simplicity and integrity. It wasn't so much what he said, but who he was, that got through to me. In spite of all my prejudices and preconceived ideas, I could not help liking him. My cynicism was disturbed by the apparent reality of his faith. For that reason alone I gave him a polite smile as I made for the door immediately after he finished.

Recognizing my tie, he started to talk to me, and we soon discovered a number of mutual friends from school, some of whom had particularly impressed me by the quality of their lives, although I couldn't have told you why. Gently but suddenly he turned the conversation. "Forgive me for asking you a personal question. You may remember that a little while ago I talked about Christianity as a friendship with Jesus. Do you know Jesus personally, or are you not quite sure about it yet?''

I was exceedingly embarrassed. In my own upper middle-class background, one never dreamed of asking such personal questions. Religion, if embraced at all, was purely a private affair. At the most one might discuss the church, usually in highly arrogant and critical terms. But asking questions about one's personal faith was like inquiring into one's private sex life: it just wasn't done.

Neatly sidestepping his crash tackle, I replied, "I've been baptized and confirmed." A good enough reply for any Anglican, I thought. But John Collins was not so easily diverted. "If I had asked those mutual friends of ours that same question, they would have said Yes immediately," he commented, with another disturbingly disarming smile.

I thought back to those friends we had discussed: Graeme, Michael, Peter. Although they had never spoken to me about Christ at school, they possessed the same sort of appealing qualities that I was beginning to find in John Collins. Logically I realized that their professed faith in Christ could have been the common denominator. The trap was tightening.

At that time, I was starting a degree course in Moral Sciences, which included philosophy, psychology, logic, ethics, and metaphysics. So I had some mental discipline in logical reasoning. Suddenly I realized I couldn't drop the subject of God and run away. I knew that this clergyman couldn't prove God. But in spite of my professed atheism, I knew that I couldn't disprove him either. Logically, it might be true or it might not be true. If God did not exist I could forget it (as I had been doing successfully for the last two or three years). But if he did exist, I had to admit that it would be the most important truth in the universe. I simply could not dismiss it as irrelevant or unimportant.

"Would you like me to explain exactly how you can find God through Jesus Christ?" asked John Collins.

I had to agree to hear him out. My scientific training had taught me that any honest seeker for truth at least ought to be open to a hypothesis, especially if it seemed even remotely important. Further, if the hypothesis appeared reasonable, however unlikely, the right action would then be to experiment, to test the hypothesis personally. This is the basis of all scientific research and the road to most forms of knowledge.

John and I decided to have breakfast together the next day at the Garden House Hotel where he was staying. We had a sumptuous feast—fruit juice, kippers, eggs and bacon, toast, coffee—because John wanted as much time as possible to explain to me the way to God. I needed that time since, although I didn't realize it at the time, I was incredibly ignorant and confused about Christ and the Christian faith.

John began by asking if I felt any need of God. I couldn't honestly remember feeling any need, apart from that impulsive cry when I was suffering from a hangover. That surely was not enough. Perhaps in my more reflective moments I was unsure of the purpose of my life. "Is that what you mean by a need of God?" I asked John. He explained that a sense of purpose is certainly included, but that our primary need of God exposes itself in our need for forgiveness. In countless ways we have broken God's laws, we have gone our own way, we have done our own thing. That is why God is naturally unreal in the experience of us all, until something is done to change that. Surprisingly, I did not need much convincing about this. I was ashamed of some things in my life; I would not like the whole of my life to be exposed. Also, I could see logically that this was a possible explanation for my sense of God's remoteness and unreality. If he did exist and if I had turned my back on him, it followed that there would be a breakdown of communication. "Yes," I said after further discussion, "I'm prepared to admit that I have sinned and so need forgiveness."

John then described the next step as believing that Christ had died for my sins. "Oh no," I thought to myself. "Here come all those religious cliches that don't mean a thing. Anyway, how can the death of Jesus all those years ago have any relevance to me today?"

Then John surprised me. He took a piece of toast and placed

it on his upturned left hand. "Let this hand represent you, and this toast represent your sin," he said. Looking at the cold, greasy, semi-burnt piece of toast, I thought it was a fair analogy. He went on, "Now, let my right hand represent Jesus, who had no sin on him at all. There is a verse in the Bible which speaks about the cross like this: "All we like sheep have gone astray; we have turned every one to his own way; and the Lord [God in heaven] has laid on him [Jesus] the iniquity of us all" (Isa. 53:6). As he quoted that, John transferred the toast from his left hand to his right hand. Then, with his genuinely winsome smile, yet with the simple triumph of a chess player's Checkmate, he said, "Now where is your sin?"

My arrogant self despised the simplicity of such an analogy, but logically it was as plain as could be. "I suppose my sin is on Jesus," I replied. In my heart I was beginning to see it, even though my mind wanted something more intellectually profound. Perhaps this was the meaning of the cross. Perhaps Jesus did somehow take upon himself our sin and guilt so that we, sinners though we all are, could be free to know the love and forgiveness of God, without any barrier at all. John reinforced the idea with several other verses in the Bible which made exactly the same point.

"Next," he said, "you have to count the cost." To put it simply, I had to be willing to put right (with Christ's help) everything that I knew was wrong in my life, and put Christ first in my life. We discussed the implications of this, and I saw clearly that if these things were true, I couldn't make a half-hearted decision. It had to be all or nothing.

So we went the final step to knowing God. John told me a promise of Jesus that I had never heard before: "Behold, I stand at the door and knock. If any one hears my voice and opens the door, I will come in" (Rev. 3:20). We talked a little more, and I saw that faith simply means taking a person at his word. If, in prayer, I asked Jesus into my life, I would be depending on his promise that he would come in and make God real in my experience.

It all seemed far too simple, and left a host of philosophical questions totally unanswered for me. But at least I understood the directions that John had given me.

"Let me suggest alternatives," he said. "Either we could go to my room and have a prayer together, or I could give you this booklet which sums up what I've been saying, and has a personal prayer at the end which you could make your own."

I was much too embarrassed to pray with him then, and anyway I needed time to think. "I'll take the booklet," I said, and rose to make a hasty retreat, muttering something about being late for a lecture.

"Just one more thing," added John. "If you decide to pray that prayer, would you write and let me know that you've done it? I would be so grateful!"

Off I went, with my mind racing. I had gone to breakfast as a humanist, and now, just an hour later, I trembled with excitement knowing I could be on the verge of a totally unexpected discovery. Either that or I'd find yet another reason for disillusionment which would only deepen my atheistic conviction.

Alone in my room that evening, I read the booklet *Becoming a Christian* by John Stott, the Rector of All Souls, Langham Place, London, where John Collins was a curate. The booklet was largely a summary of our breakfast conversation, and with all its simplicity it was compellingly clear and logical. Steadily I realized that if these things were true, I really wanted them to become true in my own life. Awkwardly I slipped onto my knees beside my bed and prayed the prayer at the end of the booklet:

Lord Jesus Christ, *I humbly acknowledge* that I have sinned in my thinking and speaking and acting, that I am guilty of deliberate wrongdoing, and that my sins have separated me from Thy holy presence, and that I am helpless to commend myself to Thee;

I firmly believe that Thou didst die on the cross for my sins, bearing them in Thine own body and suffering in my place the condemnation they deserved; *I have thoughtfully counted the cost* of following Thee. I sincerely repent, turning away from my past sins. I am willing to surrender to Thee as my Lord and Master. Help me not to be ashamed of Thee;

So now I come to Thee. I believe that for a long time Thou hast been patiently standing outside the door knocking. I now open the door. Come in, Lord Jesus, and be my Saviour and my Lord for ever. Amen.

Absolutely nothing happened. No visions, no feelings, no experiences, nothing. Everything seemed just the same as before. I felt let down; and yet as I climbed into bed I had a quiet sense of peace that I had done the right thing.

The next morning I still felt no different. But, I thought to myself, what if Christ really had come into my life? Shouldn't I trust his promise, at least for a day or two, to see if anything would happen? I wrote a note to John Collins to say that I had done it, and asked him, "What happens now?"

Two days later I received his encouraging reply. His note also mentioned that he was asking a friend of his to call on me. "Oh no!" I thought. "I really have fallen into a religious trap." *I definitely did not want to become religious.* But when I found out the identity of John's friend, my attitude altered completely.

For years I had been a cricket enthusiast and a player, though not a great one. Of my various cricket heroes, none was greater than David Sheppard, who had recently been captain of Cambridge, Sussex, and all-England teams. On numerous occasions I had seen him play: a magnificent opening batsman whose command of the game was totally exhilarating. So I was astonished, and pleased, when I found this hand-written note on my table the day I received John's reply:

John Collins wrote this morning suggesting that I look you up. I will look in after lunch, but do not stay in especially.

Yours,

David Sheppard

2
Finding Christ at Cambridge

"I DON'T THINK I HAVE EVER MET ANYONE who was so confused!" was David Sheppard's comment about me a few months later. Looking back I see now that my religious ideas were like a ball of wool after a playful kitten had been hard at work: an incredible tangle of various beliefs, interwoven with a few strands of Christianity here and there. Interestingly enough, a few weeks before I went up to Cambridge a very good friend of mine had given me *The Imitation of Christ* by Thomas à Kempis, and I had found the book both moving and stimulating. It created in me a measure of spiritual hunger. But my knowledge of the gospel was effectively zero.

I later discovered that I wasn't the first or the only spiritually blind person. Jesus once said to a thoroughly religious and intelligent man, Nicodemus, "Truly, truly, I say to you, unless one is born anew, he *cannot see* the kingdom of God" (John 3:3). The brilliant university scholar, Saul of Tarsus, said much the same thing: "The unspiritual man does not receive the gifts of the Spirit of God, for they are folly to him, and he is not able to understand them because they are spiritually discerned" (1 Cor.

2:14). In more recent times, the eminent philosopher Bertrand Russell wrote a book called *Why I Am Not a Christian,* but it is clear from this book that he had little or no understanding of the basic truths of the Christian faith.

David Sheppard invited me to come to his rooms at Ridley Hall, an Anglican theological college in Cambridge, where he was in his final year prior to ordination. Almost every week throughout the academic year I went over to talk to David, often for as many as three hours at a time, and he began to lay a foundation for my faith. He helped me grasp the only foundation that will stand firm against every wind of doctrine and storm of life, the foundation of Jesus Christ. Each week we read a passage of the Bible that David had carefully chosen to meet my particular need at that stage: Psalm 103 on assurance; Psalms 32 and 51 on repentance; Isaiah 53 on the Cross; Luke 24 and 1 Corinthians 15 on the resurrection; James 1 on temptation; John 17 on prayer; Romans 12 on service; and so on.

It is impossible to stress how vital these sessions were for me. Humanly speaking, I would never have survived as a Christian without them. My first question after asking Christ into my life was, "How on earth will I be able to keep this up? Won't it be like those useless New Year's resolutions all over again?" My Confirmation and various other attempts to turn over a religious new leaf had also been failures. This time at Cambridge I didn't realize at first that, through the Spirit of God, I had started a new life. Then came two slender inklings of this reality: first, my Army habit of swearing at about every fifth word ceased immediately; second (and much more important), a new love for people slowly began to dawn in my heart.

I certainly needed this new love! I had been an appalling snob, and must have been even more unpleasant in the eyes of other people than I am now! To begin with, I was proud of my family background. I had a long Scottish pedigree, my "family tree" having been carefully researched back to the 11th century. The Watsons lived for many centuries in Saughton, Edinburgh. However, one branch of the family moved in 1537 to the Lake District in northern England. Until World War One our family home was Calgarth Park, at one time a 3,000-acre estate developed by Richard Watson, my great-great-grandfather.

Richard Watson was an able and colorful character. He was born in 1737 and went to Trinity College Cambridge in 1754. At the age of 27, he became professor of chemistry in the University, although he admitted later in his own *Anecdotes,* "At the time this honor was conferred on me I knew nothing at all of Chemistry and had never read a syllable on the subject, nor seen a single experiment in it." After fourteen months of study in Paris, however, during which he once destroyed his laboratory with an explosion, he returned to Cambridge to deliver "a course of chemical lectures to a very full audience." He wrote numerous scientific papers and was promptly elected a Fellow of the Royal Society of Science.

Only three years later, in 1771, the chair of divinity, considered by Richard Watson "the foremost post of learning in Europe," became vacant. He studied divinity for one year and was unanimously elected to the chair of divinity. Of Watson's prolific writings, probably his most important apologetic work was *Apology for the Bible,* published in 1796 in answer to what he called "the scurrilous abuse of the Scripture" contained in Thomas Paine's *Age of Reason. Apology for the Bible* was particularly well received, although when he handed it to King George III it is believed that the King retorted, "I never knew that the Bible needed an apology!" The King made Watson Bishop of Llandaff, Wales, which was the poorest bishopric in the country, but was considered by many of Watson's contemporaries to be his stepping-stone to Canterbury. Then Watson clashed on a point of conscience with both William Pitt and George III, who subsequently kept him at that safe distance in Wales, where he remained for 34 years.

Coming from that background I went to school at Wellington College, where my father, uncles, and cousins all had been educated, and then joined the third regiment of the Royal Horse Artillery, which was rightly proud of its traditions and outstanding military achievements. Understandably perhaps, I had thoroughly embraced what the Bible critically calls "the pride of life," a human vanity based on privileges of birth or personal achievement, a vanity which can prove a considerable stumbling block to a true knowledge of God. The apostle Paul acknowledged that "not many of noble birth" had been called by God (1 Cor. 1:26). In fact, God "opposes the proud, but gives grace to the humble" (James 4:6). These were painful and humbling lessons I slowly began to learn.

This new life that I had received needed much nurturing, and God met that need particularly through David Sheppard, whom I respected enormously. It was mostly through David's influence that I began to overcome some of my entrenched prejudices. Gently he encouraged me to get involved with the Christian Union in my college, St. John's. I found this extraordinarily difficult. Not only was the whole experience of Bible studies and prayer meetings totally foreign to me—I had no idea that such things existed and was shocked initially by the religious intensity of them—but on the surface I had nothing whatever in common with the other Christians in my college. They came from backgrounds very different from mine, and our interests were widely different as well. I was studying philosophy, and played hockey or squash seven days a week; most of them were studying chemistry, and played no sport at all. (Today I find such differences quite irrelevant—what Christians have in common in Christ gloriously transcends any worldly distinctions.) I almost had to be pushed into fellowship with my Christian brothers, since I was afraid of becoming a religious fanatic by associating with them. I vividly remember one young man gripping his chair in such agony when he prayed that I genuinely thought he was suffering from serious constipation. "What if my fellow army officers could see me now!" I found myself thinking.

I wasn't the only person worried. I'm not sure what I wrote about all this to my mother, but she was clearly a little anxious when she found out I had become religious, especially after the tragedy with my father. Later I was summoned to meet with various family friends and relatives to assure them that I wasn't rushing off to become a monk! My army friends were frankly puzzled. They couldn't quite imagine the young officer who had gotten drunk in Hamburg nightclubs now sitting in Cambridge prayer meetings. "It will soon pass," they said charitably. "Everyone goes through these phases during college. He'll probably be a Communist next term!"

But it didn't pass. Certainly I went through some agonies of doubt. A short time after my conversion I wrote in my diary, "Is it all true, or am I making it up?" David Sheppard obviously saw that I was going through a difficult time, and he chose Psalm 103 for us to read together that evening:

> *Bless the Lord, O my soul;*
> *and all that is within me, bless his holy name!*
> *Bless the Lord, O my soul,*
> *and forget not all his benefits,*
> *who forgives all your iniquity,*
> *who heals all your diseases,*
> *who redeems your life from the Pit,*
> *who crowns you with steadfast love and mercy,*
> *who satisfies you with good as long as you live*
> *so that your youth is renewed like the eagle's.*

My intellectual questions remained unanswered, but the Spirit of God used this psalm to reassure me of God's love, and I was quietly conscious of his never-failing presence. The whole thing seemed so *right and true.* Here, I was convinced, was something of the "unsearchable riches of Christ" that countless millions of men and women have discovered down through the centuries. I worshiped God, my Father, through Jesus Christ, my Lord and Savior.

I knew, of course, that my faith needed to go beyond pure devotion and involve my intellect. My philosophy lecturers gave no help. If they mentioned God at all, they did so cynically, treating the subject as a curious historical debate that philosophers used to take seriously before this age of logical positivism and linguistic analysis. To them the issues of today had long outmoded any medieval fantasies about God. I was fortunate, however, to have as my psychology supervisor Malcolm Jeeves, a deeply committed Christian who helped me integrate my faith and intellect. I began to understand the basic difference between the meaning and the mechanism of something. For example, even though a "conversion experience" can be described in psychological terms, this in no way invalidates the meaning or significance of it.

I also came to see that all the different forms of knowledge depend, at least in part, on faith. One example is logical or mathematical knowledge: providing I accept by faith the fundamental principles of mathematics, I can gain further knowledge by sheer logical reasoning. Another example is scientific or experimental knowledge: providing I accept by faith certain laws of science, I can gain further knowledge by testing hypotheses with empirical investigation. There is also personal knowledge, or the knowledge of persons, which is quite different from either mathematical or scientific knowledge. You can never "prove" a person. You can only know a person, and you can know a person only if you commit yourself to the time and energy required of a relationship with that person. I realized that the same was true of knowing God. I saw that no scientific world-view, however complete it may one day become, could give us a knowledge of God.

An important milestone in my struggling faith came when I helped my best friend to find Christ himself. Tom was a delightful person—amusing, generous, gifted in sports, and in every way charming. Within a week or two of my own conversion David Sheppard had taught me how to lead someone to Christ, and so I shared what I could with Tom, who was obviously interested. I am sure that I put it rather badly, but through the help of a visiting preacher, Maurice Wood (now Bishop of Norwich), Tom accepted Christ into his life. I was so overjoyed I literally could not sleep a wink all night, and I have never lost that sense of deep joy and immense privilege that comes through helping someone find God. Tom joined me in my weekly sessions with David Sheppard, and I found all this a huge encouragement.

I could see, however, that Tom was still cautiously weighing the cost of true Christian discipleship. For him, the account in the Gospels of the meeting between the rich young ruler and Jesus was all-important. Tom was disturbed by the clear instruction Jesus gave to that man to sell everything he owned before he could follow him. I told Tom that I was sure this instruction did not apply to everyone (I was much too threatened myself to imagine that it did), but that riches were the special idol in that young ruler's life, and therefore he needed an unusual and particular challenge before Jesus could be his Lord as well as Savior. Tom, however, took this command of Christ both literally and seriously. In order to follow Christ with integrity, he thought, he would have to give up everything. Perhaps, like most of us, Tom needed to face particular issues in his life from God's perspective. Tragically, over that first Christmas vacation Tom found the continuous round of social engagements too appealing, and seemed to surrender his faith.

I have no doubt that Tom was being thoroughly honest with himself. He rightly hated hypocrisy. But now we found, having agreed to share rooms together soon after his conversion, that we disagreed on what was fast becoming the most important element in my life. Although we still remained very good friends, I personally found this an extremely testing time, and found that it increased my resolve to put Christ first, whether others came with me or not.

Partly for these reasons I developed a fairly disciplined faith from the start. Having overcome some of my initial culture shock at the "fanaticism" of those who took the Christian faith seriously, I began to order my life according to rules that I set myself. Every morning, without fail, I would read my Bible and pray for at least forty-five minutes. Every day I prayed for people and needs from my rapidly growing prayer list. Every week I memorized six verses from the Bible, together with their references, and reviewed the ones I had previously learned. I began to devour Christian books, reading concurrently a doctrinal, a biographical, and a devotional book, in order to feed on a balanced diet. I was committed to Christian fellowship (though I found prayer meetings difficult for a long time) and active in evangelism, taking many friends to evangelistic services and seeing some of them come to Christ.

On the negative side I was equally strong. Having tasted the bitterness of some of the forbidden fruits in the world, I decided not to smoke (not that I did anyway), not to drink, dance, go to cinemas or theaters. Now that I had tasted the new wine of the Spirit, the old wine of the flesh seemed like lukewarm water, and I spat it out of my mouth. Some of those standards were certainly too legalistic, but to this day I am grateful for that note of discipline in an age when such words are no longer fashionable. It provided a rock-like foundation, on which the superstructure of my Christian life could later afford to be more flexible.

Of course, not everything was quite as pious and simple as it may have seemed. For all my new-found fervor, the one event that I dreaded was an open-air service organized by the Christian Union, to be held at the Mill at the end of summer term. The Mill was a popular pub by the river where most of my pagan friends spent their Sunday lunches drinking beer. On a sunny day there was always a crowd there, the target audience for the Christian Union's open-air service. But however real my ardor for Christ had become, it unquestionably did not stretch to soap-box oratory before my beer-drinking friends. "Will you be there with us?" pressed my Christian brothers. "I'm not sure yet," was my evasive reply. Imagine my relief when another friend invited me to lunch in his rooms for that very same Sunday. His sister would be there, and I had a sneaking suspicion that this friend hoped I might fall in love with his sister. She was a delightful girl anyway, so I readily accepted the invitation. What a perfect excuse for missing the open-air meeting! Much to my surprise, however, when I arrived at my friend's rooms that Sunday he said, "It's such a glorious day, let's get a punt at the Mill and go for a picnic."

We arrived at the Mill, which was now thronging with students, including many from the Christian Union who were conspicuous in their Sunday best. When some of them saw me they were thrilled. But clearly they were not so thrilled when I climbed into a punt with my friend and his sister, and pushed off for a picnic. Even worse, when we were some distance down the river towards Granchester, my friend (always a tactician) made some excuse about having work to do and jumped off the punt to run back to his rooms. That left me alone with his sister, wondering how on earth I was going to get back to the Mill later without losing face entirely with my Christian friends. There was no way out of it; so back we came, like any other romantic couple on the river that day, arriving at the Mill when the evangelistic thrust of the open-air meeting was at its climax. I suspect that I became the object of some fervent prayer for the next few weeks, and my promising friendship with this charming girl came abruptly to an end. No doubt, in my embarrassment, I had been ungracious and rude to her. It's not an easy job adjusting to new life in Christ.

Churchgoing was something of a hurdle also. It had always been a terrible chore for me: penance which I assumed Christians thought necessary to atone for all their many sins. Escorted by David Sheppard, I began to go to various services where the form was usually familiar to me, but the spirit was altogether different. I had never before seen so many young people of my age singing hymns and praying prayers as though they really meant them! And the sermons, although sometimes in a biblical jargon which I found incomprehensible, were most informative, personal, and helpful. I was horrified however by the first evangelistic sermon I heard only a few days after my conversion. That was far too much hell-fire and judgment for my liking. So when I saw long lines of undergraduates going up to the preacher afterwards to say that they had accepted Christ, I was astonished, and relieved that I had done it quietly on my own earlier in the week. Never in a thousand years (I thought), would I have joined such a line of inquirers. Later I began to be utterly enthralled by the constant proclamation of the gospel by visiting preachers every Sunday evening in Holy Trinity Church, and I totally failed to see why some of the many friends I took with me could not embrace Christ there and then.

My first Christmas vacation proved to be another important milestone, for two main reasons. First, I had the tremendous joy of leading my mother to Christ. We had never talked together with ease about personal matters; but her second marriage, after my father's death, had not been an easy one, and for many reasons she was aware of her need for God's help. Very simply I outlined the steps I had taken to find Christ, and I prayed with her, phrase by phrase, as she asked Christ into her life. It was wonderful to see her begin to read her Bible and pray, and I could soon see the difference that Christ was making in her life.

Then, after Christmas, I went as a leader to a boys' camp run by the Rev. E.J.H. Nash, affectionately known as Bash. David had had to apply some pressure on me before I agreed to go, as I had planned to go on a skiing holiday with Tom and two other male friends of ours and four stunningly beautiful girls, one of whom was Britain's top model at that time. I suspect that David saw this as a real and obvious temptation for me, the flesh fighting hard against the Spirit. The Spirit won—but not without a struggle.

After my leadership experience at school and in the Army I felt sure that I was just the kind of leader these boys needed, so I looked forward to organizing some activities for them. In fact, I spent almost the entire time peeling potatoes, sweeping floors, and scrubbing pots and pans. Imagine doing that instead of skiing with four beautiful girls! However, that camp and the next one at Easter taught me a vital lesson: that humble service is the essential basis of all Christian work and ministry (see the example of Jesus washing the dirty, smelly feet of his disciples). I also experienced there a quality of warm, accepting Christian fellowship with sane, intelligent, and vivacious contemporaries, that I had never imagined possible. That fellowship, together with the brilliant short talks given each morning and evening, quite convinced me of the reality and richness of the Christian faith. I had stumbled onto a priceless hidden treasure, as Jesus once described it, and I realized that no sacrifice was too great to obtain it.

3

Grappling with
Theology

WITH DAVID SHEPPARD AS MY SPIRITUAL MENTOR, perhaps it was
obvious that I would think in terms of ordination. I had arrived
at Cambridge with no clear plans about my future. I had
vaguely thought of a career in diplomacy or the Foreign Office,
but it had all been a distant dream. What about ordained ministry in the Anglican church? David asked me if I had considered
it.

The decision, however, was not clear-cut. Some relatives and
friends of my family were not enthusiastic. For them, ordination
was only for those who could not think of anything better to do.
"I suppose if you became a bishop it might be all right," commented one. Better wisdom came from some older Christians
who were beginning to know me. Fearing that I might simply be
copying the example of David Sheppard, they strongly suggested the teaching profession instead. "There is a lot of excellent work you can do as a Christian teacher," they said; and
indeed I had thoroughly enjoyed a term teaching at Wellington
College just before going to Cambridge.

The primary obstacle to ordination, though, was a personal

one. I was terrified at the thought of speaking in public. Shouting orders to a troop of soldiers on parade was one thing; the thought of preaching a sermon almost paralyzed me with fear. The first talk I ever gave on the Christian faith lasted for a nightmarish five minutes. My mouth was dry, my knees were knocking, my hands shaking. I thought I would never make it to the end. But it wasn't just the delivery that bothered me. "The trouble is," I protested to David, "I wouldn't know what to preach about." "More likely," he countered, "when you really begin to know your Bible, you won't know what *not* to preach about!" I was far from convinced.

Then on Trinity Sunday 1955 I attended a service in King's College Chapel for the first time. I am not sure why I went, except that most undergraduates visit at some time or other because of the beauty of the building and the excellence of the choir. I enjoyed the aesthetics of the occasion, but what riveted my attention was an unemotional but powerful sermon on the need for men in the ordained ministry. I had absolutely no idea who the preacher was, but later discovered that he was the Rev. Cyril Bowles, now bishop of Derby. Through him God spoke so directly to me that my call to the ministry, which had been growing slowly stronger as the months passed, was now abundantly clear. I applied to the selection board of the Church of England, and was accepted as a candidate for ordination.

After two years studying philosophy, psychology, logic, ethics, and metaphysics, in which I had done reasonably well in spite of my increasing preoccupation with Christian work (and my involvement in sports), I changed my major study to theology. As a very young Christian I found most of the lectures difficult and disturbing. I discovered that it was theology, and not philosophy as Keats had suggested, that could "clip an angel's wings, unweave a rainbow." Much of the dry, dusty stuff that we were studying seemed thoroughly destructive, and seemed to have no apparent connection with the knowledge of God. The theological scene wasn't entirely bleak. The saintliness of Professor Charlie Moule shone radiantly through his lectures, and significantly he began each series with humble prayer, submitting himself to the authority of God and his Word. I admired Professor Owen Chadwick for his immense scholarship, combined with a gentle and dry sense of humor. And Professor Henry Chadwick made the theological controversies of the early church live in an astonishing way, impersonating the fathers and heretics as though he had known each one of them.

However, apart from these, few lecturers spoke with any conviction. One dear man, who was insufferably boring, began most of his sentences like this: "It is not unreasonable to suppose that it might not be the case that these two events were not unconnected." I would often have to count the negatives on my fingers, to find out whether the final statement was positive or negative. In my own reading, Matthew's comment about Jesus, at the end of the Sermon on the Mount, came home with fresh force: "When Jesus had finished this discourse the people were astounded at his teaching; unlike their own teachers he taught with a note of authority" (Matt. 7:28-29 NEB).

In sweeping contrast to the dithering caution of most of these academic theologians, who were efficiently undermining the faith of some of my friends, Billy Graham led a mission to the university in November 1955. Interestingly, when he tried, somewhat unsuccessfully, to be academic, his preaching lacked power. But when he accepted the apparent foolishness of the message of "Christ crucified" and preached it with simplicity and integrity, the power of God's Spirit was manifested and changed the lives of many undergraduates. It was a lesson I have never forgotten. In addition, once I had worked through the vital question of accepting the authority of Scripture as the Word of God, it became and has remained my constant desire over the years to build, and never undermine, faith. I could understand well the complaint of Goethe, a self-confessed agnostic, who once said to a preacher: "You tell me of your certainties; I've enough doubts of my own."

Of course any preacher or theologian may go through times of agonizing doubt, even over the most basic issues of the gospel; but if he does, he should share these with a few friends, not preach them from a pulpit or publish them in paperback. I was a curate in Cambridge when John Robinson's book *Honest to God* came out. It seems that it was written during some "dark night of the soul" in John Robinson's life, and related some of his deep questionings. Perhaps he had no friends close enough to turn to at the time. In any case such doubts published in popular book form did untold damage. When the psalmist was totally baffled by God's seeming inactivity in the face of suffering, he wisely kept silent: "If I had said, 'I will speak thus,' I would have been untrue to the generation of thy children" (Ps. 73:15). He knew that declaring his doubts publicly would have helped no one.

G.K. Chesterton's words are still very much to the point, in an age when it is fashionable for some preachers to express their humility by saying how much they do not know: "What we suffer from today is humility in the wrong place. Modesty has settled upon the organ of conviction, where it was never meant to be. A man was meant to be doubtful about himself, but undoubting about the truth; this has been exactly reversed."

It would be wrong to conclude that I thought my theological studies a waste of time. Apart from the enormous gain I received from Professors Moule, Chadwick, and Chadwick, being forced to think through carefully most of the basic issues of the Christian faith was invaluable to me: To what extent can the Bible be trusted as the Word of God? What is the nature of its inspiration and authority? Why is the cross so central to the faith? What was the atoning work of Christ? How convincing was the evidence for the resurrection? Indeed, how sure can we be about anything, concerning matters of faith?

When preparing for an essay I would receive a long list of books to read, and I knew that likely some of them would contain pointed intellectual attacks on basic Christian truths. I would then ask one or two academic theologians whose personal beliefs were similar to my own for another list of books on the same subject, written by scholars taking a much more positive and orthodox view. Then I would read books from both sides and try to balance my essays with arguments and counterarguments. It was hard work, but in this way I tried seriously to tackle the critical questions without being "tossed to and fro by every wind of doctrine" or theological fashion. Through this process I became even more convinced intellectually of the great themes of the Christian gospel, and this was important for healthy growth in Christ. I was learning to love God with my *mind* as well as my heart and soul and strength. During this time I also held on to a shrewd principle that someone once voiced to me: "Never let what you don't know shake your confidence in what you do know." I certainly didn't have the answer to every intellectual question, yet all the time I clearly was growing in my knowledge of Christ.

Undoubtedly the most formative influence on my faith during my five years at Cambridge was my involvement with the boys' camps, or "Bash camps" as they were generally known. During those years I went to no less than 35 of these camps: two at Christmas, two at Easter, and three in the summer of each year. These were tremendous times for learning from the other leaders the very basics of Christian ministry. Through patient and detailed discipling (although that word was never used), I learned, until it became second nature, how to lead a person to Christ, how to answer commonly asked questions, how to follow up a young convert, how to lead a group Bible study, how to prepare and give a Bible message, how to pray, how to teach others to pray, how to write encouraging letters, how to know God's guidance, how to overcome temptation, and, most important, how to laugh and have fun as a Christian—how not to take myself too seriously. I also received excellent grounding in basic Christian doctrines, with strong emphasis on presenting them with clarity and simplicity. All this was being constantly modelled for me by those who were much more mature in the faith, and I may never fully realize how much I owe to the personal help that I received over those five years. No Christian organization is perfect, of course; naturally our strengths can often be our weaknesses as well. But if God has given me an effective ministry in any area today, the roots of it were planted during those remarkable camps. It was the best possible training I could have received.

Sadly, I was not so receptive to learning what my theological college, Ridley Hall, could teach me during my two years there. Largely through my own fault this was a difficult and negative time. With the combined influence of the Christian Union at Cambridge and the boys' camps, I had developed strong evangelical convictions, and was thus deeply suspicious about everything else within the Christian church. In my spiritual immaturity, my faculties had not yet been "trained by practice to distinguish good from evil" (Heb. 5:14). I disliked the formality of Ridley chapel services every day; I rejected any teaching that I considered remotely "liberal"; I found the staff giving theoretical answers to questions I was not yet asking. My foremost priority was still the evangelistic work I felt called to do in the university, which I often did at the expense of activities at Ridley Hall, most of which I regarded as an interference. The Ridley staff members were patient with my spiritual arrogance and critical attitudes, and I am sure now that, had I been a little more humble and positive in my approach, I would have recognized what these Christians had to offer and grown far more in my knowledge of God. I have since met many students at theological colleges and seminaries of all traditions who are as critical and defensive as I was, digging in with their own convictions for safety and not being open to other ways God may be at work within his world-wide church. Such an attitude is inevitably a mark of immaturity.

At the same time, serious questions are today being asked (and rightly so) as people try to develop the most helpful methods of training men and women for the ministry of the church. More emphasis is being placed (and in my opinion still more is needed) on offering first-hand experience in church work as part of the training. This was the method of Jesus who lived and worked with his disciples. They watched him on the job, listened to him, went where he sent them, reported back to him, learned from their mistakes, and so on. It wasn't "first theory, then practice." The learning and doing were closely interwoven. The disciples were called primarily to be "with him," and in this way they were prepared for the most effective leadership that the church has ever known. There are surely lessons here for every theological college and seminary.

My own first-hand training for ministry came during my first curacy in an environment thoroughly different from Cambridge. John Collins, then vicar of St. Mark's Church, Gillingham in Kent, invited me to be his curate. So, from the cultured atmosphere of Cambridge I moved, almost five years after my conversion, to the tough dockyard parish in Gillingham.

4
Curacy
in a
Dockyard Parish

"YOU'LL ESPECIALLY ENJOY THE YOUTH CLUB," John Collins told
me. "David MacInnes has done an amazing work there!"

David MacInnes, whom I had met at Cambridge and liked
very much, was the bachelor curate who had joined John and
Diana Collins when they began their work at Gillingham two
years before I came. For financial reasons David and I lived in
the Victorian vicarage, together with the Collins's and their two
young children, a Swiss *au pair* girl, and Graham Scott-Brown, a
brilliant young doctor who was preparing to go to Nepal as a
missionary. It was quite a group! We had a marvelous time praying, planning, studying, and working together. Much was
beginning to happen in the parish, and so almost every day there
were developments to encourage us or battles to be fought.

It was a privilege to enjoy such close fellowship together. We
avoided the loneliness that snares many Christians working in
tough situations, and we certainly had lots of fun with each
other. For instance, with various meetings occupying us almost
every evening until quite late, John, David, Graham, and I
used to cook a light supper for ourselves after Diana had wisely

retired to bed. I became an expert at omelettes (and nothing else), and later calculated that I must have cooked at least 1,000 omelettes during my three years in the vicarage. For one week we tried to vary the menu with cauliflower-cheese made in a pressure cooker; but Diana protested that the smell wafting upstairs was like the British army taking its boots off, so back we went to omelettes!

I quickly discovered that the studio apartments David and I occupied just inside the front door were also the main meeting rooms for parish groups: Confirmation Candidates, Young Wives, Pathfinders, Sunday School, Mothers Union, Youth Fellowship, Christian Night-School, and so on; and because of the shortage of stackable chairs, my first six months in the parish seemed largely taken up with moving forty chairs several times a week, back and forth from the hall five hundred yards down the road to our respective rooms. At times I wondered, was I ordained for this? I began to see that it was a part of humble service, much like scrubbing those pots and pans at the boys' camps, and ever since then I have looked for willingness to serve in simple, menial tasks as an important qualification for spiritual leadership.

David MacInnes had done a magnificent work in the youth club, although I soon saw that John was stretching the point considerably when he said that I would enjoy it. Always this ministry was challenging, and after the meetings we could have a good laugh. At times I was simply terrified, although I tried hard not to show it. David had attracted some lively gangs of teddy-boys (as they were then called), who thought nothing of having a good fistfight or carving one another up with razors, broken glass, switchblades, or any other weapon handy. (This was not what I was used to at St. John's College Cambridge.) David had a terrific sense of humor which these tough fellows— and girls—obviously enjoyed, and because of this he was able to exercise effective control without antagonizing potential troublemakers to the point of violence. He won the respect of virtually everyone who came to that club—we usually had about 140 there each Friday evening—and his fifteen to twenty minute talks during the epilogues at the end of each evening were quite brilliant. I was only too glad when David was there running the club, with me playing a minor role, and I felt distinctly inferior whenever he was away. Every Friday, before going down to the club, I would get on my knees and pray over this and other relevant verses from Jeremiah 1: "Be not afraid of them, for I am with you to deliver you, says the Lord" (Verse 8).

During my three years at Gillingham we never actually had a fight in the club, but several times we came very near to one. One night when David was speaking at a different meeting, I noticed two rival gangs present at Youth Club, each with about twelve to fifteen members. I kept a close watch on them, but when I was in another room talking to someone else, the two gangs slipped out of the exit. "There's a fight brewing outside!" I was told. So I rushed out of the door to find the two gangs lined up on either side of the small courtyard at the bottom of the steps. They were ready to charge at each other and were equipped with a variety of ugly weapons. Without thinking I raced down the steps into the middle of them, and, with an authority which surprised even me, I told them that on no account could they fight on these premises, since this was a Christian club. I was obviously in a highly vulnerable position, but they accepted my word and, after a few tense minutes, walked away. Later I heard, with much sadness, that they had gone to a nearby park and fought a pitched battle there, several of them ending up in the hospital.

Although I'm not sure that I ever "enjoyed" the youth club, we had some hilarious moments, often at the expense of visiting speakers. We had a few battered sofas and armchairs which were pulled up to form the front row of an audience for the epilogue, and inevitably some of the fellows would pull out long chunks of upholstery stuffing, which they would push into their ears as soon as the speaker started his talk. Also, if we failed to get all cigarettes extinguished in time for the talk, someone would blow huge smoke rings across the speaker's face. These rings were always fascinating to watch as they floated in front of us all, and they were guaranteed to upset all but the most gifted speaker.

Others at the meeting would stuff their pockets with billiard balls and roll them noisily across the bumpy wooden floor. Occasionally a small coin or piece of foil would be inserted at the bottom of a light bulb, so that when the lights were turned on, the fuses blew.

Every summer we would take seventy or eighty for a week's camp. The majority of those who came had already been won for Christ through the club, but God never eliminates personalities when he saves people, and unfortunately for David and myself some of the young people were great practical jokers. We found that often the jokes were neither practical nor funny, at least not for us! Our cars regularly disappeared, or had their wheels removed. I had everything put into my bed from black coal to damp sand to live frogs. Whatever else could be said about the youth club, it was never, never dull. Most of the families in Gillingham had moved originally from the east end of London, and it was the sharp cockney wit which kept us on our toes all the time. Yet these weeks were always magnificent. I developed an enormous affection for numerous individuals and families, and it was wonderful seeing the power of Christ changing the lives of so many.

Of course there were casualties, in more ways than one. When one dockyard apprentice found Christ, he was beaten up by his co-workers in the dockyard the next day and was in the hospital for four days. Thankfully he stood his ground well, and today he is a fine Christian leader. Others had too close an identity with the group from which they were converted, and although we spent numerous hours with them, the pressure of the group proved too much and they fell away from Christ. We also made the mistake of allowing quite young Christians to give their testimonies of conversion. Often they had committed almost every crime in the book before their conversion, and therefore their stories were both dramatic and popular. But those who gave their testimonies invariably went through spiritual attacks later, and some tragically gave up their faith. There were many disappointments in this youth work, but Christ became real for many, and they reached out as a result: we often took small teams to other youth clubs for effective evangelistic evenings. On the whole we were the toughest and liveliest club for a wide area, so our visits to other groups were always popular. Ministering, sharing, and laughing together with our young people, David and I found that our time and effort were always profitably spent.

In countless other ways I had much to learn about ministering. Giving short talks at a camp for schoolboys (as I had done at Cambridge) was quite different from preaching in a large Victorian church in a dockyard area. Here both John and Diana Collins were superb tutors. Diana, who was trained as an actress, worked hard on my voice, trying to change it from the sound of an Army officer shouting orders on parade to something more fitting for a pulpit. She had me relaxing on the floor and then making all sorts of extraordinary noises which reverberated around the vicarage, much to the amusement (or annoyance?) of the others who lived there. I found her exercises an enormous help, and I find it sad that so few preachers have any guidance concerning the use of the one "instrument" they are playing all the time.

John also gave me invaluable training—his curates have always been known as some of the best-trained clergy in the Church of England. After every sermon I preached, John would take the time and trouble to comment thoughtfully on both the strong and the weak points. He never made more than three critical comments on any one sermon (even if he could think of thirty-three), so that I was never discouraged. Indeed, he was a great encourager, and with his and David's preaching setting an extremely high standard for me, I found during these years the best training that I could have found in any parish. Time and again I was astonished to hear from friends who were curates in other parishes that very few received any practical training at all, and all too often they lacked encouragement as well. Both John and Diana are marvelous enablers, spotting the potential in others and working hard to develop that potential to its fullest. They have realized that the work of training others is perhaps the most important work that any Christian leader can do.

Doubtless it is largely for that reason that the churches they have served have been unusually blessed by God.

Ministering together in Gillingham was frequently rewarding and lots of fun, but it was never easy. At times it could even be dangerous. One night we were attacked in the vicarage by a wild and drunk Irishman. He was well-known in the area for allegedly shooting at his wife with a double-barreled shotgun, but fortunately missing. We had given shelter to his wife and children in the past and the man had often been belligerent. On this occasion he was convinced for some reason that we were sheltering his wife again. Although we assured him that we were not, he broke two windows in the vicarage, smashed down a door or two, and by the time the police arrived our assailant was armed with a huge boulder. Inside the vicarage we were pretty scared and had armed ourselves as best we could. I had a broomstick, John a baseball bat, and Paul Russell (David MacInnes's successor) the ebony statue of an African girl. Diana, more resourceful as always, was in the bathroom upstairs pouring pitchers of cold water on the man's head as he tried to smash his way through the front door. In court later on, the man said to the judge, "Your Honor, I remember it was raining at the time!"

Among other outstanding memories of that first curacy, a week's visit from that remarkable and courageous Dutch woman, Corrie ten Boom, was definitely a highlight. Knowing that she would be staying with us in the vicarage, we were all a little nervous because of her reputation and her amazing ministry, not only in Ravensbruck Concentration Camp, but throughout Germany after the war. God had used her particularly to release many people from satanic powers. The Nazi reign of terror had been literally a devilish inspiration, partly through the leaders' heavy involvement with the occult. Hitler often referred to being guided by voices within him, and he was surely devil-inspired, if not devil-possessed. So, with Corrie's record of helping those who had been troubled by evil spirits, we just wondered what she might find in our English vicarage! As it transpired, Corrie was the most wonderful, gracious, and compatible guest we could possibly have imagined. It was hard to think of her suffering all the brutalities of a Nazi concentration camp. She seemed so gentle, so good, and so filled with delightful humor. Her talks, illustrated by simple yet unforgettable visual aids, made a lasting impression on us all. Best of all, she was someone who walked daily with her heavenly Father: sometimes in conversation, while we were expressing some anxiety about something, she would turn so naturally to prayer that it took us a few moments to realize she was talking no longer to us, but to God.

When John, David, and I were seeing her off at a crowded Gillingham train platform, Corrie wanted to say something to us that we would remember. As the train moved slowly out of the station, she stuck her head out the window and shouted to us, "Don't wrestle, just nestle!" All eyes turned towards us, three clergymen formally dressed in clerical collars with faces turning delicate shades of pink. I have never forgotten that simple slogan, even if in practice I haven't always found it easy to rest quietly in the love and peace of the Lord. I'm convinced that God wants all of us to develop a simple trust in the Father's loving care, a trust that Corrie learned through appalling suffering and grief.

After three years of excellent and varied training at St. Mark's, Gillingham, I went back to Cambridge for my second curacy, deliberately accepting an invitation to a totally different parish for the purpose of widening my experience. I had no idea that the next three years at the Round Church would combine some of the most thrilling, confusing, traumatic, and painful experiences of my life.

5
Spiritual Brokenness & Renewal

FROM THE VERY START IN CAMBRIDGE I unexpectedly became depressed. It was not a severe depression but even though I had exchanged the relative ugliness of a dockyard town for the outstanding beauty of Cambridge, the finest university in the world (I may be a little prejudiced), I missed the vitality of Gillingham more than I had imagined possible.

Mark Ruston, my vicar, whom I had known well from my previous five years in Cambridge, could not have been more thoughtful and caring at the time, and his steady and faithful ministry for Christ has been one of the outstanding features in Cambridge for more than twenty-seven years. However, in sharp contrast to the lively wit of Gillingham, Cambridge as a town seemed remarkably dull. Even the church services, compared with those at Gillingham, seemed dull. Parish prayer meetings felt the same: heavy and depressing. I have never been very patient, and I was aching for some spark of life, a little enthusiasm, something, whatever it might be, to make God seem more real in our midst. There was nothing wrong with the teaching; it was simple and biblical, and obviously helpful to scores of people. But oh, for some of the fire of the Spirit!

Looking back, I believe that God used my youthful impatience to spur me into a series of personal studies that proved a major turning point in my life and ministry as a Christian. I started to read the great histories of revival, fascinated by the outpourings of God's Spirit on groups of men and women at different times and in different places. Many of the manifestations of revival were totally strange to me, with people prostrate before God, weeping and crying out to him for mercy, sometimes for hours on end. It was hard to distinguish the sovereign work of the Spirit of God from human hysteria or infectious enthusiasm. But clearly something remarkable had happened in the era of Jonathan Edwards, John Wesley, and George Whitefield in the eighteenth century, and during the Revival of 1800, the Awakening of 1858, the Welsh Revival of 1904, and the Hebrides Revival of 1949, not to mention numerous others. I began to pray seriously that God would send us another revival even here in Cambridge, and I sometimes joined forces with others who shared my burden such as the Rev. Herbert Carson, Vicar of St. Paul's, and Dr. Basil Atkinson, Senior Librarian at the University.

Next, I studied again the Acts of the Apostles, and felt the conviction steadily dawn on me that a normal spiritual dynamic present in the early church was almost entirely missing within the church of our day. Even in Gillingham we seemed to have been on a spiritual wavelength altogether different from what was recorded in Scripture. I remember our staff there studying 1 Corinthians 12 and 14, where the apostle Paul writes fully about the gifts of the Holy Spirit, especially prophecy and tongues. We simply had no idea at all what he was talking about.

We had taken the usual evangelical line that all such gifts were purely for the apostolic period and were not meant for today. But why then were such specific instructions for their use given within the pages of the New Testament? And what about those strange Pentecostals, whose growth particularly in South America had been one of the most remarkable Christian movements of this century? Had these Christians experienced power and gifts of the Spirit that we were somehow missing? These became the insistent, urgent questions that I could not escape.

As I studied Acts, I was also doing a detailed Bible study on the nature of faith. I could see in example after example that God's unusual demonstrations of power came when men and women dared to take him at his word, whether they understood it all or not. For example, in the Christmas story the Virgin Mary is promised the gift of a son who would be "the Son of the Most High." Puzzled, she asks, "How shall this be, since I have no husband?" (Luke 1:34). Once again the angel gives the promise: "The Holy Spirit will come upon you, and the power of the Most High will overshadow you" (Luke 1:35). So she accepts the promise of God at its face value, and responds in two very important ways. First, she surrenders her life completely to God. "Behold, I am the handmaid of the Lord; let it be to me according to your word" (Luke 1:38). And then, amazingly, she begins to praise God that the promise is *already true,* even though the reality of the actual experience is still to come. In the *Magnificat* or *Song of Mary* (Luke 1:46 ff.), she bursts out in praise:

My soul magnifies the Lord,
and my spirit rejoices in God my Savior,
for he has regarded the low estate of his handmaiden.
For behold, henceforth all generations will call me blessed;
for he who is mighty *has done* great things for me...

As far as Mary is concerned, it is already true.

With that and other examples of faith, I began to realize how often we limit God to our own narrow human understanding, or else to a specific scientific world view. I wondered, why shouldn't we take him more seriously at his word, whether we understand it or not, whether we immediately experience it or not?

Most significant of all in my study, I began a series of meditations in the Beatitudes from the Sermon on the Mount. I had been inspired to do this after reading two volumes of expository sermons on Matthew 5–7 by Dr. Martyn Lloyd-Jones. I found that over a period of three to four months God was taking me through the first four Beatitudes in my spiritual experience. It was a painful and humbling business.

Blessed are the poor in spirit (Matt. 5:3). The Greek word for "poor" is a strong word meaning poverty-stricken or bankrupt. It comes from a word meaning "to cringe." So the text describes a man so overwhelmed by a sense of poverty that he is beaten to his knees and has to throw himself on the mercy of God.

This was a far cry from my own opinion about myself. After a fairly successful first curacy, I was coming to the conclusion that I had more or less arrived. I was well taught in Christian doctrine and practice, and thought it was my life's task to preach the truth and to correct those who disagreed with me! Apparently I also had enough confidence in my own discernment to make judgments about the dullness and heaviness of the services at the Round Church. So God began to rebuke me for my spiritual pride, my arrogance, my self-righteousness, and my critical spirit. As he took away those masks, I painfully began to see myself as I really was, as he saw me—and I did not like it. Instead of looking at the speck in my brother's eye, I started to look at the log in my own eye. On my knees alone before God, I had nothing to boast about, and much that caused me shame, though I had become skilled at hiding this from others and even from myself. I suddenly saw that I was the one who was poverty-stricken, and I found this a most uncomfortable disclosure. I realized that if I was really in earnest about revival, it had to begin in me.

Blessed are those who mourn (Matt. 5:4). Again, the Greek word for "mourn" is a strong word meaning "lament." If I dropped a glass and it broke into many pieces, the Greek word I could use to describe the scene is the root word of "mourn." Blessed are those who are shattered. Why are they shattered? Because of their poverty of spirit. There is natural logic in these Beatitudes: the first leads directly to the second, and so on.

As I meditated on this statement by Jesus, I began literally to weep for my spiritual poverty. I saw my low level of faith, my lack of love for Jesus, the poverty of my love toward others. I saw that it was precisely for such sins that Jesus had been crucified on the cross, and that by my sinful attitudes I was grieving the Spirit of God. Grief is a love-word: I knew that God still loved me more than I could possibly imagine, but I saw much in my life that hurt him, and the knowledge of that broke me. More deeply than ever before I began to repent of everything that I knew was wrong in my life.

Blessed are the meek (Matt. 5:5). The meek person is someone who is mourning so deeply for his spiritual poverty (see the verses' logical progression again) that he is willing unconditionally for God to do what he wishes in his life. The meek person will not protest or complain; he will not dictate his terms; like the Virgin Mary he will say, "Let it be to me according to your word." Now that I felt broken at the foot of the cross, I was willing for God to have his own way in my life, whatever that meant, and however painful it might be. When Mary surrendered her body to become the mother of Jesus, she didn't know what this would mean in coming years. Simeon later warned her that "a sword will pierce through your own soul also" (Luke 2:35) an apt description of her agony when Jesus was crucified. God brought me to that point of meekness where I was genuinely willing to say, as far as I understood it, "Not my will, but yours be done."

Blessed are those who hunger and thirst for righteousness (Matt. 5:6). Broken at the cross, mourning for my spiritual poverty, I found I had a consuming desire to be right with God, to be filled with his Spirit, to glorify him in every area of my life. I spent much time in prayer, asking God to do something new in my life. Never before had I known such hunger for God. With Jacob I said in my heart, "I will not let you go, unless you bless me." Time and again I asked God specifically to fill me with his Spirit, knowing from my study of revival that the Spirit of God often revealed himself in tremendous power, falling on men and women in such a way that they were either struck on the ground or filled with "inexpressible joy." I was willing for anything to happen, but nothing did. I was disappointed, perhaps a little disillusioned, but the hunger never abated. All this took place during the winter months of 1962–63, some time before anyone said anything about "charismatic renewal." However at that time, prayer groups for revival, which I took as a mark of the Spirit's activity, were springing up all over the place. Often the groups would spend half the night or all night in prayer, such was the increasing hunger for God among a good many Christians. Paralleling my own spiritual search, my previous parish, St. Mark's Gillingham, had been holding nights of prayer for revival; and at one of these (I think in February 1963) those who were present were gently aware they were being filled with the Spirit. They entered into a new experience of the love of God. Some of the toughest most uncultured and unlettered men and women had fallen in love—with Jesus. There was no doubt that God had done something new and wonderful within the congregation. Significantly, it happened shortly after I had left the parish! My expectation increased that God would meet with me also.

Suddenly I realized the missing link. I had been praying and praying to be filled with the Spirit, but when nothing seemed to happen I assumed that my prayer had not been answered. As I shared this with a friend, I remembered the example of the Virgin Mary. Once she accepted God's remarkable promise to her, she began to praise God that it was already true, even before the promise was confirmed in her experience. I had been waiting for the experience *before* I would believe that the promise had been fulfilled. That was entirely the wrong way around. I had to claim the promise of the Spirit's filling, believe it to be true, start praising God that it was true, and let the reality or experience of the promise follow in God's own way and in God's own time.

Once again, I confessed every sin I could remember committing, including my unbelief, and asked God for forgiveness. I told him that I was willing to obey him, whatever the cost. I then asked him to fill me with his Spirit, *and began to praise him that he had now done it.* As I went on praising for perhaps ten to fifteen minutes, I had a quiet but overwhelming sense that I was being embraced by the love of God. There were no startling manifestations. I did not speak in tongues, and anyway I still believed that this gift had died away with the apostles. But it seemed that the presence of God filled the room in which I was praying. I *knew* I had been filled with the Spirit, and I was bubbling over with new joy.

I went straight over to see my dear friend Dr. Basil Atkinson. "Basil," I said like someone bursting with good news. "I've been filled with the Spirit!" "Praise the Lord!" replied Basil spontaneously, and we had a wonderful time of praise and thanksgiving together.

The next day I went to a clergy meeting in Cambridge, and with the same exuberance I said to one of my colleagues: "Peter, I've been filled with the Spirit!" Poor Peter did not know what to say. Nervously he looked out of the window. "I think it may rain today," was his comment, and he moved along to talk to someone else about funeral fees, or some such business. I began to realize that I had to choose carefully when to speak. It had to be the right person, the right words, and the right time. But God had met with me in a fresh way—of that I was certain. It was hard being silent about it.

6
Baptism
or Fullness?

EVERYONE IN LOVE TENDS TO SAY and do stupid things at times. No doubt I made many mistakes in the time after my new experience, for I was in love with Jesus in a way I had never known before. I devoured the Song of Solomon, that exquisite love poem in the Old Testament. As a beautiful analogy of the love relationship between a believer and his or her Lord, it expressed what I felt in the depths of my heart. I spent even more time in prayer, mostly praising and worshiping God, and at times his presence was so real to me that I opened my eyes expecting to see him transfigured there in front of me. I read the Bible as never before, and certain passages leaped out at me as though they were alive. They all seemed like love letters from God. In personal evangelism I had never experienced such fruitfulness: now for months I had the joy of leading four or five people to the Lord almost every week! I loved people with a new quality of love, and found many opportunities to share what God had done in my life, especially with those who were hungry for him.

But what exactly *had* God done in my life? The reality of it all was unmistakable and undeniable, but how could I understand it in biblical and theological terms?

I began six months or more of furious study trying to grasp from the Scriptures what it was all about. Three friends and I went for counseling to someone whose ministry we respected immensely and whose concern for revival was well known, Dr. Martyn Lloyd-Jones. He began our day with him at Westminster Chapel by asking us to share our testimonies, since over the last few months we all had known a fresh working of the Spirit of God in our lives. Obviously the testimonies had personal variations, but they were significantly the same. To our surprise, Dr. Lloyd-Jones then shared a very similar testimony of his own, telling of the Spirit coming upon him shortly after the Hebrides Revival in 1949, through the ministry of Duncan Campbell. He said that this experience had given him a new authority in his preaching ministry. Then, as we talked a little further, he said, "Gentlemen, I believe that you have been baptized with the Holy Spirit."

To be honest, I was not happy with that expression, and to some extent never have been, if it refers to something subsequent to conversion. But the Doctor (as he was often called) was quite adamant in his preaching on this theme. Less than two years before our meeting, on May 25, 1961, the Doctor had said in a sermon:

> There are some who are guilty of quenching the Spirit by limiting in their very thinking the possibilities of life in the Spirit...I am convinced that there are large numbers of Christian people who are quenching the Spirit unconsciously by denying these possibilities in their very understanding of the doctrine of the Spirit. There is nothing, I am convinced, that so quenches the Spirit as the teaching that identifies the baptism in the Holy Ghost with regeneration. But it is a very commonly held teaching today. Indeed it has been the popular view for many years. They say that the baptism in the Spirit is "non-experimental," that it happens to everybody at regeneration. So we say, "Ah, well, I am already baptized with the Spirit, it happened when I was born again, it happened at my conversion; I've got it all." Got it all? I simply

ask, in the name of God, why then are you as you are? If you have got it all, why are you so unlike the New Testament Christians? Got it all? Got it at your conversion? Well, where is it? I ask.

A fair question! It summed up perfectly my own feelings about a shallow doctrine of assurance that can lead all too easily to complacency. I understood that we are justified in the sight of God the moment we put our trust in Jesus. But I also knew that we should normally be experiencing the "fullness of life" that Jesus promised us. My three friends and I had seen in ourselves little evidence of the spiritual wealth we have as individuals and as a church, once we are in Christ. The Spirit's recent renewing work in us, whatever term we used to express it, seemed to be his waking us up to the normal New Testament Christian life.

The Doctor, while rejoicing in what God had done, warned us of certain dangers, notably that a doctrine of sinless perfection could creep into our thinking. In the past, when men and women had been blessed by the Spirit (whatever they called this blessing), they sometimes claimed that they were so dead to sin and so full of love that it was no longer possible for them to sin. After the great Baptist preacher Charles Spurgeon heard a man teaching such nonsense at a conference one evening, he poured a jug of milk over the man's head at breakfast the next morning. By the man's unholy reaction, the doctrine of sinless perfection was speedily disproved!

In my own case, the filling of the Spirit had nothing to do with any claims to sinless perfection, but the whole spiritual dimension had become more real to me. My life with God had been going up and down (in obedience, attitudes, etc.) at a fairly low level of reality; now I found that God was more real, Jesus more real, prayer more real, the devil more real. I was still going up and down, but on a new level of reality. I definitely had not arrived. I was anything but perfect. Indeed one or two unexpected lapses into sin jolted me out of any self-satisfaction. If I had been renewed in the Spirit, I also needed a constant, daily, fresh renewal. I could take nothing for granted.

This was a period of much heart searching, diligent study,

and discussion with others. Because of the growing number of people in the country claiming to be filled or baptized with the Spirit, John Stott was asked to give a paper clearly spelling out the biblical doctrines. This he did with his usual clarity, authority, and graciousness, but taking a diametrically opposite view to the one put forward by Dr. Martyn Lloyd-Jones. In what became his booklet *The Baptism and Fullness of the Holy Spirit,* Stott wrote: "According to Scripture we have been baptized with the Spirit because we have repented and believed . . . I would appeal to you not to urge upon people a baptism with the Spirit as a second and subsequent experience entirely distinct from conversion, for this cannot be proved from Scripture."

What was I to make of this "clash of the Titans," as a friend of mine once described it? Which view was right? Had I (and others) been "baptized in the Spirit"? If not, what had happened in our experience?

The expression "to baptize in the Holy Spirit" comes only seven times in the New Testament, six of them linked with the baptism that John the Baptist said the Coming One would bring (Matt. 3:11; Mark 1:8; Luke 3:16; John 1:33; Acts 1:5, 11:16; 1 Cor. 12:13). John had come to baptize with water as a sign of repentance, but Jesus would baptize with the Holy Spirit to introduce people into the blessings of the New Covenant. At Pentecost this promise was fulfilled, and the event was repeated only in the house of Cornelius as the Gentile equivalent of Pentecost. As Peter explained, "And I remembered the word of the Lord, how he said, 'John baptized with water, but you shall be baptized with the Holy Spirit.'" Peter went on, "God gave the same gift to them [Gentiles] as he gave to us *when we believed in the Lord Jesus Christ"* (Acts 11:16-17). Repentance (Acts 11:18; cf. 2:38) and faith are thus the only necessary conditions for a person to be baptized in the Holy Spirit.

From those six references it seems clear that the baptism in the Holy Spirit refers to Christian initiation. It is the spiritual event by which all people are brought into Christ, whether Jew or Gentile. This is even more clear in the seventh reference: "For by one Spirit we were all baptized into one body—Jews or

Greeks, slaves or free—and all were made to drink of one Spirit" (1 Cor. 12:13). Nowhere is it suggested that Christians are, or can be, baptized in the Spirit after their conversion to Christ. Indeed, "Any one who does not have the Spirit of Christ does not belong to him" (Rom. 8:9). Nor is it suggested that Christians should wait or pray for the baptism of the Spirit. The first disciples had to wait for the initial outpouring of the Spirit at Pentecost; but after that, the "promise of the Spirit" was for all those who repented and believed.

The trouble with speaking of the baptism of the Holy Spirit as a second-stage experience for some Christians (as the Pentecostals and many charismatics do) is not only that it cannot be proved in the New Testament, but also that it becomes divisive. The Christian church is then split into the have's and the have-not's, leading to the inevitable dangers of spiritual arrogance on the one hand and resistance to the Holy Spirit on the other. The truth is that we have "every spiritual blessing" in Christ (Eph. 1:3), and there is nothing further that we have to seek beyond Christ. This is what John Stott taught so clearly, and I believed and continue to believe that this is what Scripture teaches.

I had to conclude, though, that the challenge that Dr. Martyn Lloyd-Jones made was a valid and important one, even though I believed that he was mistaken in describing a post-conversion experience as a baptism in the Spirit. My study and observation since then have borne out that theologically we may have everything in Christ, but this is not always evident in our lives. How many of us today have the vitality and joy, faith and love of those first disciples? The fact is that the actual experience of what we already have in Christ may come to different people at different times and in different ways. We can compare a person's deepening experiences in Christ to the unwrapping of a multiple parcel—Paul significantly talks about the "unsearchable riches of Christ." What someone is and has in Christ may become a reality in his experience at various stages. When a person is overwhelmed by the love of Christ, is filled with new praise, and finds fresh joy in prayer, in the study of Scriptures, and in personal witnessing, it is understandable if he speaks of this experience as the "baptism of the Spirit," even if, as we have seen, that is not the scriptural meaning of that phrase.

The tragedy is that, because of others' unscriptural use of language, many Christians have held back from those riches in Christ that the Holy Spirit is renewing today in the church. But we cannot choose such an alternative. We cannot settle for a dull orthodoxy or a low level of spirituality. We need to be open to all that the Spirit is doing in our midst. We have not yet entered into the "glorious liberty of the children of God." All of us have much more of our inheritance in Christ to experience, and we should always remain hungry and thirsty for him.

Most Christians would agree that we all need to be continuously filled with the Spirit, since that is the plain injunction of Scripture (Eph. 5:18). Many believe and teach that this filling is purely a matter of "imperceptible growth into Christ." That is not, however, the testimony of countless Christians all over the world who have experienced some form of spiritual renewal, whatever it may be called. A diocesan youth chaplain wrote to me, "I was aware of the need of something more from God...One day I received the Spirit through prayer and the laying on of hands...I felt the Spirit pour in until it seemed I must burst...For how many years I had been longing for joy! And now it came, joy that welled up within and issued in praise and thanks and adoration to a glorious God. Love also began to appear...Christ was more real and more loved. The Scriptures came alive in a new way." This man has developed a powerful and gracious ministry since his personal renewal. His story is not unique—hundreds of thousands of people have similar ones to tell.

Something happens, therefore, when men and women are filled with the Spirit, something that can transform their lives and their ministry. Their churches may come alive in a way not known before. In our western Christianity we have become so cautious about experiences because of their obvious dangers that we tend to rule them out altogether. However, no one can read the pages of the New Testament without seeing that they are shot through with specific and often dramatic experiences of the Spirit. It is the church's comparative lack of these today that evidences her desperate need of renewal. Although it is important that we get our terminology right, we must not allow our debates about terminology to stifle our hunger for God and our openness to the Spirit. If we believe the expression "to baptize with the Spirit" denotes initiation into Christ, we must not exclude the serious possibility of further significant steps of renewal that we can term "being filled with the Spirit," "receiving the Spirit," or "experiencing the release of the Spirit." We all need much more of what God longs to do by his Spirit in our midst.

Anyway, at the same time as many of us were coming to terms with the different viewpoints expounded by Dr. Martyn Lloyd-Jones and John Stott, news was coming to us from North America about Episcopal and Lutheran churches that were being renewed in the Spirit as we had been. However, most of the Americans testified to speaking in tongues (a love language of praise in the Spirit) which had not been my experience at all. Several British Christian leaders and I met in London with several of these people who came across the ocean to share their stories with us. To be honest, some of them impressed us very little. We sensed that they had simply been born again, and their abundance of stories and absence of theology left us far from satisfied. Others were more impressive, and what we heard from them certainly indicated that something was happening; but whether it was genuinely a work of the Spirit or some Satanic diversion from the true heart of the gospel was not always easy to discern. One man, at an extravagant Hilton Hotel luncheon for Christian leaders, was introduced as "the greatest Spirit-filled Christian in the world today" (applause from the platform party). This kind of attitude did not go down well with us conservative English clergy. It was a puzzling period in our lives.

In particular, we were confused by this new emphasis on tongues, together with some reference to prophecy and healing. During my theological studies I had become a dispensationalist—I followed the teaching of such men as B. B. Warfield, believing that all such gifts, whatever they were, were purely to establish the truth of the gospel with "many wonders and signs" during the New Testament period. I believed these gifts were definitely not for today. However, at a conference for evangelical clergy some months before the Americans' visit, I had heard Dr. Edwin Orr speak on his specialized subject of Revival. It had been a fascinating day, and I remembered one of his points in particular. Tracing quickly through the history of revival, he had pointed out that each significant revival within the church brought back something lost since the days of the early church. He also had predicted that the next revival would bring back certain gifts of the Spirit that largely disappeared after the first few centuries of church history. Looking back later on these ideas, I began to wonder, was this what God had been doing through the Pentecostal movement since the turn of the century? Was this what he was beginning to do again—introduce these gifts into the historic churches which had unitedly rejected them earlier and thus forced the Pentecostal church to come into being? What was the scriptural teaching about these gifts? Were they really for today after all?

The more I studied the New Testament the more I became convinced that the teaching that these gifts were only for the apostolic age was no more than a rationalization for the long absence of such gifts in the church. The biblical arguments for this teaching were thin and questionable, and I could see that all the gifts could be just as edifying in the church today as they were in the first century, and many of them could give as effective an evangelistic thrust to the church today as is recorded in the Acts of the Apostles. Of course in the early church a "foundational" level of prophecy was necessary for the completion of Scripture, and since Scripture is now complete this level is unnecessary and therefore not to be looked for. But in the New Testament church many other levels of prophecy helped build up the believers, so why shouldn't they be part of our resources today? I could not readily understand the value of tongues, except that, especially with my new longing to worship and praise the Lord, I often felt frustrated by the limitations of language. My spirit often wished to transcend expression in ordinary syntax. I felt this need equally in intercession, when I did not know exactly what to pray for but felt a strong burden to pray for someone at a given moment in time.

Such thoughts developed in my mind over a period of about six months, by which time I had started to "earnestly desire the spiritual gifts," according to the command in Scripture (1 Cor. 14:1). Once during those months a dear couple laid hands on me and prayed for me for a whole hour, asking that I would be given the gift of tongues. For the first five minutes I prayed with them. For the next five I could only think, "What *would* some of my colleagues say if they could see me now?" And for the next fifty minutes I prayed that this couple would stop praying. Eventually I won, and the whole experience was not particularly helpful for me. I suppose I was expecting God to waggle my tongue so that the words would rush out. But that never happened to me. A while later I was struck by Luke's statement in Acts 2:4 that *"they*...began to speak in other tongues, as the Spirit gave them utterance." They had to do the speaking. I realized that the Spirit normally does not take us over in the way an evil spirit may.

So I asked God to give me a language in the Spirit through which I could worship and praise him. I began to praise him in English and then let my mind relax while my spirit went on praising with the first syllables that came to my tongue. They could have been any syllables; there was nothing special or mystical about them. After about thirty seconds I stopped. "David, you're just making this up!" I said to myself. Then I thought, what if God had answered my prayer? What if I had been speaking in tongues? At the very least I should go on for a little longer. I was sure that God would not be angry with me if I were doing the wrong thing; he knew that I genuinely wanted to praise him as much as I could. So I went on "making these noises" for thirty minutes or more. Every time I listened carefully to the sounds, I found them most unedifying. But every time I used the sounds to concentrate on the Lord in worship, I found myself unusually refreshed. Was this what Paul meant when he wrote,

"He who speaks in a tongue edifies himself" (1 Cor. 14:4)? I cannot pretend that all my problems about tongues were solved from that moment onwards. I was deeply concerned about the integrity of what I was doing, and I wanted to be *sure*. But increasingly I found the gift to be a natural and helpful part of my daily devotional prayer life, a marvelous way of abiding and resting in the Lord.

My thinking about tongues has solidified since those early experiences. All language is simply the use of various sounds or syllables as vehicles of communication. When my spirit is praying to God, who is Spirit, I need not be confined to those sounds that happen to form my native language. Any sounds or syllables will do, providing that they are genuine vehicles of communication between my spirit and God's Spirit. Of course in public I must use sounds that everyone understands. But in private that need not be the case. Every Christian acknowledges the importance of silent prayer, or "sighs too deep for words." Why not a spiritual language which the mind may not understand? Tongues are not irrational, but transrational or suprarational. God is so much bigger than our own rational thinking. Therefore, Paul concludes, "I will pray with the spirit [i.e. in tongues] and I will pray with the mind also [i.e. in a known language]; I will sing with the spirit and I will sing with the mind also" (1 Cor. 14:15).

Because of the novelty of all this, I told only a tiny handful of friends, in strict confidence, that I thought I was beginning to speak in tongues in my private prayer life. I was living at a Biblical Research Center at the time and I knew that such news could easily be misunderstood by those around me. Imagine my concern therefore when I was suddenly asked to leave that center and find other accommodations. When I made a direct inquiry, I was told the reason: the committee responsible for this center had heard that I was speaking in tongues. This threw me into a dilemma. Was I becoming heretical? Was all this a deception of the devil? Was I in danger of leading others astray if I spoke openly about this? To whom could I turn for wise counsel? It was not an easy period in my life, to say the least, and once more I had to go back to the New Testament to gain a better understanding of the nature of spiritual gifts. Meanwhile, however, the gift of tongues was constantly refreshing whenever I used it as a genuine prayer language for the Lord.

When I found myself unexpectedly homeless, Mark Ruston graciously took me in, and I tried to continue my work with him in the Round Church much as before. I was anxious to be utterly loyal to Mark and to the ministry of that church, yet I naturally longed to share something about the renewing work of the Spirit that I had experienced. Obviously I chose to say nothing about tongues or any of the other controversial gifts. I continued running the children's church, which had been my special and enjoyable responsibility; I continued preaching at the normal services; and I began to become more involved in the work among students. Whatever private misgivings Mark may have had, he showed patient and steady acceptance of me as a person, for which I have always respected him.

Nevertheless, in our country as a whole during the sixties, a growing number of evangelical leaders showed opposition towards this renewal movement. Various well-known leaders wrote to me, urging me to "renounce tongues" publicly. One man even offered me a "plum living" in the south of England if I would make a simple but clean break from all these things. A number of letters that I received hurt me deeply. But if I had received a genuine gift from the Holy Spirit of God, how could I possibly renounce it? Would I not be opposing God and quenching his Spirit?

The heart searching continued as I went over the biblical ground for my new convictions again and again. I did not *know* I was right. Perhaps I was wrong and my critics were right after all. However, I knew it could never be right to go against one's own conscience. All I could do was commit the whole matter to God and ask him to lead me in his way, whatever the cost might be.

At the same time another form of heart searching was beginning to develop which took me equally by surprise.

7
Marriage—
A Desperate Start

It was Christmas Day 1963. The Christmas morning service had just finished, and I was standing with Mark Ruston at the Norman porch of the Round Church saying happy Christmas to each member of the congregation. A very attractive girl suddenly caught my eye. "Have we met before?" I asked. "I don't think so," she replied with a trace of a Scottish accent. "My name is Anne MacEwan Smith, and I'm a nurse at the maternity hospital on Mill Lane."

I had always mistrusted the romantic sentiment of "love at first sight," but the vibes were undoubtedly there on this occasion. Later that day, during the whole drive from Cambridge to my mother's home in Eastbourne, I could think of little else except Anne MacEwan Smith. That brief encounter had made a deep impression on me.

I was thirty at the time, and since my conversion more than nine years before I had considered carefully the advantages of the celibate life. The apostle Paul was strong on this theme: "I want you to be free from anxieties. The unmarried man is anxious about the affairs of the Lord, how to please the Lord; but the married man is anxious about worldly affairs, how to please his wife"(1 Cor. 7:32). Since my conversion I had devoted most of my time and energy to the work of Christ. David MacInnes and I had often discussed the matter of marriage, and we could think of very few advantages in getting married. We were both confirmed bachelors, I thought. And I believed a bachelor was a man who never made the same mistake once.

Two facts weakened my resolve, however. The first was that David himself became engaged! I felt somewhat betrayed, yet secretly happy for him, and I gladly accepted his invitation to be best man. The second fact was that, to my surprise, I felt I wanted to get married myself. The time seemed right.

I tried not to think too much about Anne MacEwan Smith in the few weeks after we met. In fact I forgot her name (but not her face!) when we next met at a church meeting. I didn't plan to rush into things, and I gather that the same idea was on her mind, but even without our efforts circumstances brought us together. Raised as a good Scottish Presbyterian, but living in England and going mostly to Anglican churches, Anne felt that she ought to be confirmed in the Church of England. She approached my Vicar, Mark, and asked if he could prepare her for confirmation. "You must see my curate," was his reply. "I am leaving shortly for a three-month sabbatical." She obeyed his instructions and came over to see me.

I had already started a series of confirmation classes, and since we were covering a carefully planned syllabus, it was necessary for Anne to catch up on the classes she had missed. Whether it was appropriate or not, I arranged to give her one or two private classes before she joined the group. At our first session I handed her an Anglican Prayer Book and asked her to turn to the Confirmation Service. Following my usual practice with all candidates I prepared, I commented, "You will find it just before the marriage service." A word of prophecy indeed!

We covered the material that she had missed, but I also gently asked her a few questions about her own relationship with Christ. She had always been God-fearing, she explained, but had personally accepted Christ as her Savior only two or three years before while training at Guy's Hospital. I asked her if she knew what it meant to be filled with the Holy Spirit, and when her reply was a little evasive I gave her a booklet on this subject which I had found helpful.

The next week Anne explained that the booklet had clarified a remarkable spiritual experience that she had recently had. While reading an article from a missionary magazine she had been powerfully challenged about her own lack of faith. On her knees, alone before God, she had asked him to give her a gift of faith. It seemed that in answer to her prayer the Spirit fell upon her and she was caught up into God's presence, losing all sense of time. When she became more aware of everything around her, she heard a strange sound and realized that she was praising God in a tongue that was foreign to her. She had never heard of speaking in tongues and feared that she might be going out of her mind. But she continued secretly to use this language because through it she experienced the presence and love of Jesus more than ever before. After reading the booklet that I gave her, she had decided to share her story with me.

As I listened to Anne, I marveled that despite the differences in our own two stories, the end results were the same. With me, this filling of the Spirit had been a long, tortuous struggle, complicated with intellectual questionings and many doubts. With Anne, it had been a sovereign work of the Spirit of God, without her knowing anything about spiritual renewal or spiritual gifts. As far as I could see, her experience was wholly authentic, and she evidently had a deep love for Jesus.

It was probably at this point that my instinctive interest in Anne began to deepen, and it increased even more when I first heard her pray in a prayer meeting. She prayed a heartfelt prayer which flowed with amazing spiritual authority, vision, and understanding. I had already been physically attracted to her, but I felt even more at one with her when we were both on our knees before God, and this, for me, was enormously important. If God were to bless any future relationship between us, I knew that Christ must be unquestionably first to each of us. And if we were not first and foremost "one in Christ," I could see no future for us as a couple. Therefore it was marvelous to feel so close to Anne when we were both consciously praying to Christ.

Anne and I soon became aware of our mutual affection, but we realized the extreme difficulty of pursuing this while I was curate of the Round Church. A bachelor curate has no privacy when it comes to a personal friendship with someone of the opposite sex, especially if the woman is a member of his own congregation. For this reason we entered a period of essential subterfuge. We knew that we couldn't be seen together in Cambridge—the news would travel everywhere within minutes—so we planned our shared free time very carefully. Sometimes, complete with my slouch hat and dark glasses, I would wait for Anne in my car outside the maternity hospital. Hiding carefully behind a copy of *The Times,* I could well have been tracking down the Pink Panther! On other days, Anne would take a bus to some prearranged place several miles outside of Cambridge and I would follow the bus in my car at a discreet distance. I'm not sure what the bus driver thought when I stopped every time the bus stopped, but the plan always worked. This skillful cloak-and-dagger courtship brought us to the point of announcing our engagement without anyone suspecting it except for a small circle of friends whom we had told in confidence. The announcement stunned not a few in the congregation, but they shared our joy. We planned to get married in the Round Church on September 19th.

I was so happy! God had both blessed me spiritually and given me a beautiful fiancée who had also experienced spiritual renewal.

As the wedding drew near, however, totally unexpected and serious problems arose. During the month before our wedding I was involved in some Christian activity in another city, and an incident occurred which, although minor in itself, seemed to oppose all the new-found joy and freedom in worship that had become so important to me. I felt a deep grief within my own spirit, and sensed that this was only a pale reflection of the much more serious grief of the Spirit of God. Whether or not I was right about this, I suddenly felt as if I was in a spiritual straight-jacket and I experienced something like a steel band tightening around my chest. I began coughing, and my cough steadily grew worse all that night, so that sleep became more and more difficult. The next day I went to a local doctor but he found my symptoms a puzzle. By this time I was clearly so breathless and ill that his office sent for Anne to take me to her parents' home. The wedding was only three weeks away.

When I returned to Cambridge I was so short of breath that I couldn't perform the simplest of tasks. Even walking down a street was a major achievement. My doctor diagnosed some form of bronchial asthma, but the treatment in those days was rather a hit-and-miss affair compared with the efficient treatment that asthma sufferers receive today. On the eve of our wedding I was so ill that Anne suggested we postpone the whole thing until I was better. Perhaps we should have done so, but with 250 guests arriving from all over the country the next morning, postponement seemed impossible. So, supported by medication, I struggled through the service and endured the reception. At one level I was blissfully happy to have Anne as my bride; but physically I was distressed and mentally I was anxious. Anne was exceedingly worried as well.

Our honeymoon was really a disaster. We went to a beautiful spot in North Cornwall, Trebarwith Strand, which we had carefully selected some months before. We were almost the only guests in a delightful hotel, and the weather for two weeks was absolutely perfect: blue skies, glorious sunshine, fantastic waves for surfing. It could not have been better. Except that I couldn't breathe! Each night was constantly interrupted by coughing; each day began with a brief struggle to a spot within fifty yards of the hotel, where we stayed all day, reading, talking, coughing, and attempting to sleep. We never got as far as the beach. We never even went for a single walk.

The nightmare continued on our return to Cambridge. On some days one flight of stairs to our small flat proved impossible for me. Anne had planned to go back to nursing to help out financially, but through an amazingly generous gift from a friend (one who did not know our situation intimately), no extra income was necessary and Anne did her "nursing" at home instead.

We tried to enter enthusiastically into our Christian work together, but this too was filled with problems. Without realizing what I was doing, I made a series of disastrous mistakes. To begin with, I attempted to make Anne into a mini-evangelist overnight by giving her a crash course in personal evangelism. I could not understand why she rebelled so strongly against this. It seemed to me that she was not interested in trying to bring people to Christ, and, since that was my primary calling, I wondered how our marriage could possibly work out. I failed to appreciate the importance of Paul's comment that only "*some* are evangelists." I am; but Anne isn't. In fact God has given her many spiritual gifts which have blessed countless people over the years, but it took me a long time to realize that God planned that as a couple our gifts and ministries should be complementary and not identical.

My next mistake came when I tried to mold Anne into the conventional clergyman's wife: a sort of unpaid curate whose job was to support *me* in *my* ministry. This meant, in part, offering constant hospitality in our flat, which for Anne was far from easy. In our living room, which was also my study, half the furniture had to be rearranged every time we entertained anyone for a meal. Worse, nearly all those who came were *my* friends and *my* contacts, not Anne's. "Supporting me" also meant that she went with me to masses of meetings and conferences at which I was the speaker, so that everyone knew at once who she was— "David's wife." Anne usually knew very few of those present and even began to lose her own sense of identity. Who was she? Was she no more than "David's wife"? What was her role now that she was married? Was she just an addition to me, another suitcase I was carrying around? Who was Anne Watson? In marrying she had chosen to lose her independence but her individuality was being taken away as well.

I saw none of this. Even if Anne had articulated the problem to me clearly, I doubt if I would have grasped what she was talking about. As it was, her defense was to withdraw into herself, often curling up on the bed in depressed silence. When I asked what was the matter, she did not answer. Often when I mentioned that it was time for us to go to this meeting or to that house, she did not come. Many times during those early months of our marriage I had to make the same apology: "I'm sorry that Anne isn't with me, but she is not too well." Outwardly I made light of it, but inwardly I was extremely worried. Mentally and physically we were exhausted, and we had allowed no space for mutual adjustment. Not surprisingly, with the hectic pace we were trying to keep up in our lives (far from successfully), Anne had a miscarriage.

Through all of this, however, we never forgot one incredible scene that we had viewed on our way to Cornwall for our honeymoon. The sky was a striking mixture of black, grey, and a violent orange-yellow—an astonishing blend of storm and sunset. Arc-ing across the whole scene, in the most vivid colors imaginable, was a double rainbow. Had a painter depicted the scene accurately on canvas I would have judged his work far too lurid to be true. But there it was before our startled eyes. Centuries before, God had set a rainbow in the sky as a sign of his covenant promises to Noah. It seemed to us that God, in that double rainbow, was giving us a double assurance of his love, whatever storms there might be in the future. With such a desperate start to our marriage, we needed that assurance. What we did not realize in those first months was how much we would need it in the years that lay ahead.

8
Enlivening a "Redundant" Church

"WHAT ARE WE GOING TO DO WITH YOU when we close you down?" This discouraging and unnerving question greeted me on my second full day of ministry in St. Cuthbert's Church, York. The questioner was the chairman of the Church Redundancy Commission, who had come with the rest of the commission to consider options for the future use of the church building. I had just arrived, believing in St. Cuthbert's future as a living church; the commission was already planning its future as a museum for York University! It seemed a parable of the popular image of the church in the mid-sixties: it was a museum, an ancient relic of bygone days, of occasional interest to historians and architects but having absolutely no relevance to the mass of ordinary people. I gave the chairman what may have seemed a typical pious remark from a young clergyman: "If anyone comes to this church and preaches the simple gospel of Christ, believes in the power of prayer, and trusts in the Holy Spirit, the building will be full in no time." Unconvinced, they told me I had one year's grace before, regretfully, they would have to close St. Cuthbert's down.

What had brought us to this place to minister? Anne and I were convinced that God had called us to York. As our time in Cambridge came to an end, we were offered four livings, each of which presented a reasonable salary and a good residence. After my happy experience in Gillingham we were particularly interested in one church in the east of London, but after considering their new pastoral scheme, seeking to unite two parishes that were completely divided by a huge railway cutting, I felt that the plan would never work, so we turned the offer down.

Then someone mentioned the little church in York. Having seen the Round Church's valuable supporting ministry to students at Cambridge, I was concerned for the new universities that were springing up throughout the country. Since most of them were thoroughly secular in their foundation, I could see that they, far more than Oxford and Cambridge, needed local churches that were relevant for students. York University had just recently started with 600 students, and no church in York seemed ready to take on this supportive role. As a few Christians in the city prayed about this, St. Cuthbert's Church had come to their minds.

For many years St. Cuthbert's had been becoming increasingly run down. Much of the parish had disappeared through a slum clearance program and in place of the rabbit warrens of tiny houses, light industry was beginning to emerge. The previous rector of St. Cuthbert's, the Rev. R.V. Bainton, had served at the church for twenty-four years, but he had suffered from poor eyesight and became totally blind during the last years of his ministry. He died tragically early in 1964, but the tiny congregation nobly soldiered on. To maintain the necessary services, the parish was annexed to Heworth Parish Church a mile away. The congregation had dwindled to about five for the 8:00 A.M. communion service, six for matins, and twelve for evensong. The total Sunday offering each week averaged about three dollars, and the majority of the year's income came through rummage sales, garden parties, whist drives, and lotteries. In this way the church itself remained barely solvent, but the fourteen-room Victorian rectory was cold, damp, dirty, and in urgent need of renovation.

When Anne and I first visited York to consider the situation, we arrived on an exceptionally cold and foggy day, and any asthma sufferer will know that fog is not the best weather for asthma. We found the rectory cold and damp with no form of heating apart from open coal fires in every room right up to the "servants' quarters" on the third floor. The church itself was heated by two coke stoves whose fumes, we were told, could be lethal when the wind blew in the wrong direction. With the fog alone (we were given warm hospitality in someone's home), my asthma was so bad that I had to spend the whole night sitting upright in an armchair because I would cough ceaselessly whenever I tried to lie down.

Other prospects we would face at York were bleak also. With the expected closure of St. Cuthbert's within the year, the church commissioners understandably decided that they could not spend any money on the rectory apart from essential repairs. Also, with the church annexed to Holy Trinity Heworth, I would not be appointed Rector of St. Cuthbert's, but licensed as curate to Holy Trinity, with responsibilities for St. Cuthbert's. My salary in Cambridge, when Anne and I were living in a small furnished flat, was $1350 a year, and that had been inadequate until the generous gift from my friend arrived, effectively raising it to over $1800. At York we would be moving to a filthy, cold, unfurnished fourteen-room house, and my salary would drop to $900 a year, a figure well below the poverty line I suspect. One or two clerical friends expressed concern about this, but apparently nothing could be done.

Friends warned us that York would be something of a "backwater" for us. We had already heard about the spiritual barrenness of the northeast, where few churches of any denomination showed signs of spiritual life (when we moved there we found that those descriptions didn't begin to describe how desperately barren it was). We were told by several Christians in York that the city was so unresponsive to the gospel that we would lose our spiritual cutting edge within three years, if we did not watch out. We had no personal links in York; and all that we were familiar with there were its cathedral (the minster), its railways, and its two famous chocolate factories.

So why did we go? We went because we believed, deep within our hearts, that God had called us there. I am not a great one for visions and revelations, and have always been impatient with those who say, perhaps a little glibly at times, that the Lord has told them to do this or that. Nevertheless, as Anne and I prayed carefully about which parish was God's place for us, realizing that every human consideration about York seemed totally negative, the strong conviction gained on us that the Lord wanted us there. In fact he gave us a promise (and I'm not a great one for being given promises, either): "I will fill this house with glory" (Hag. 2:7, AV). Clinging to that promise, at times by our fingernails, we moved to York on July 1, 1965.

Our first task was to make at least one or two rooms in the rectory habitable. Fortunately Anne had some experience in this, and with the skilled help of a friend we decorated my study and an upstairs sitting-room within two weeks. After that, the pace slowed down considerably, primarily because of our lack of funds. Out of my $900 salary we had to buy two space heaters, purchase a duplicator for the parish, and scavenge as much second-hand furniture as we could. Family and friends helped quite a bit as time went on: my parents-in-law advanced their will to us, enabling us to buy carpeting and curtains; my mother moved from a house to a flat, giving us what she no longer needed; Mark Ruston's mother did something similar; my uncle released old family portraits, trunks, and packing cases from storage; and when families living near us in York bought new furniture we gratefully took their throw-outs from them. In this way, the fourteen rooms gradually were furnished, even if not always to our taste!

From the beginning, we found the tiny congregation of St. Cuthbert's very welcoming, and we started to form friendships which have continued and deepened ever since. Most of the people were Linfoots: Dan Linfoot (the churchwarden), Florrie Linfoot, Barbara Linfoot, Harry Linfoot, Ethel Linfoot, Doreen Linfoot, Michael Linfoot, Ethel Linfoot. When in doubt I said "Linfoot!" Then there were Mrs. Lunn, Mr. and Mrs. Barrett, Mr. and Mrs. Brown, Mr. and Mrs. Lancaster. They were all the salt of the earth, but there were not many of them. We visited in the parish trying to establish relationships and tell people about the love of Jesus. We found these Yorkshire people blunt but friendly, although virtually no one understood why we were visiting. Some assumed it must be for money, and a few gave us a dollar or two hoping to encourage us. None seemed interested in God's free gift of his Son and as far as I know no one came to our services as a result of our visiting.

Preaching was initially a great strain for me. I prepared my sermons as thoroughly as I could and tried to deliver them with spirit (whether mine or God's, I am not sure). However, the moment I stepped into the pulpit I could see most of the congregation switching off; they had just done their bit with the hymns and psalms, and now it was the clergyman's turn to do his. With rare exceptions, they simply did not listen. It reminded me of that jingle:

The color of our curate's eyes
I cannot well define;
For when he prays, he closes his;
And when he preaches, I close mine.

One of my early series of sermons was titled "Abraham, a Man of Faith." I knew if anyone at St. Cuthbert's needed the faith of Abraham, I certainly did, so each week I couldn't wait to hear my next week's sermon! I also believed that God's Word is always powerful and over the months I watched joyfully as the hearts of some within the congregation opened up to God as flowers open to the sun. A few, I discovered later, had probably found a living faith in Christ many years before, largely through the ministry of the York City Missioner. However, their faith had been frozen deep inside them for a long time, and it had to be brought out of that deep freeze and given time to thaw before it came to life again. Others had never understood the gospel of Christ. One or two did not want it or could not accept it, and eventually left us; but others slowly, very slowly, found the light of Christ penetrating the darkness within them, and they became strong Christians. They formed a vital core of the congregation for many years to come. As in Gillingham and Cambridge, we saw the gospel of Christ change the hearts of individuals in York and we learned at the same time the New Testament truth that faith and patience go hand in hand.

Anne and I knew, of course, that if we wanted God to do anything among us, we must give time to serious prayer. On my first Sunday I announced we would hold a short meeting for Bible study and prayer at the rectory on Thursday. We chose to meet in my study, the one room we had decorated so far. About four or five showed up, one woman accompanied by her dog. After giving a short and simple Bible study, I mentioned some needs and encouraged everyone to pray a few short prayers. I prayed, and there was a long pause; Anne prayed, and there was another long pause. I prayed again, and Anne prayed again. So we all said the grace and went home. It certainly didn't hint of revival, yet in time our Thursday Fellowship became quite the most important event in our church life. Without it the Sunday services and everything else would have lacked the vitality of the Holy Spirit. Repeatedly I emphasized to the congregation the absolute importance of those times of corporate study and prayer, and eventually the people's response was tremendous.

At the beginning, when nothing much seemed to be happening in the parish, Anne and I felt God calling us to more sustained periods of prayer. We had no children at that time, and we had very few meetings to attend, so it was easy for us to do something about this call. We chose to spend most of every Wednesday in prayer and fasting. During that time we worshiped God, read the Scriptures together, prayed about everything in the parish, and asked for God's guidance. We knew that in any church there are always 101 good things one can do. But our question was, what does God want us to do in our church at this moment in time? Through these days of prayer, which we kept up for the best part of a year, we gained a sense of God's direction for his work and saw significant results develop in the church.

One of our immediate concerns, of course, was the matter of

giving. At my first church council meeting, someone asked if we could hold a gift day some Saturday. I responded warmly to the idea, saying that I would be in church all day and would ask people to spend a few moments praying as well as giving. Some of the church council members, however, thought quite differently. They said that people would be too busy to come into church to pray, with all their weekend shopping to do; but if I were to stand in my cassock at the bus stop near our church and shake a tin cup in my hand, a few coins might be given. They also suggested we might get several dollars by stringing a big sheet between two trees, and encouraging passersby to toss a coin or two into it.

This was, I think, the only time I ever resolutely refused to do what the church council proposed. I insisted that I would be in church, inviting people to pray as well as give, and if they were too busy to say even a short prayer I was not very interested in their gifts. I was convinced we had to have the right attitude about giving because God looks first and foremost for the love of our hearts, not the offer of money. If the gift of money, or anything else for that matter, is a genuine expression of our love and thanksgiving to the Lord, it becomes a part of the worship that glorifies him. Nothing can be a substitute for that love relationship that God wants us to enjoy with him in Jesus Christ.

The council eventually acquiesced to my ideas after a brief struggle. I don't think that any previous gift day had yielded more than $20. This one yielded $122 which for that tiny and dispirited congregation was astronomical! Over the years we never had appeals, and the rummage sales and whist drives soon died a natural death. Instead, each year on the Sunday before Harvest Thanksgiving, I would preach from the Bible about the principles of giving. The following Friday we would have a special time of prayer, often half a night of prayer (in addition to the Thursday Fellowship), and on both Saturday and Sunday people would come with their thank-offerings to the Lord. Our second year the total was $321, the next year it was $450, the next $617, then $1388, $1555, $1680, $2385, $3172, $5552, $6231, $7664, and so forth. All these were designated specifi-

cally for missionary support, not for the work in York. Throughout the years the weekly offerings rose steadily too, and we
occasionally had extra gift days to meet special expenses caused
by the expanding work. Even so the offerings never reached
what they could or should have been; we had much to encourage
us, but nothing to make us complacent.

The first visible evidence of change and growth in the Sunday
services came after we had been there six months. At that time
we began holding a family service in place of the traditional
matins service one Sunday morning a month. Then, three
months later, we decided to use this format for our morning
service every week. I had been impressed by the value of family
services both in Gillingham and Cambridge, and felt that St.
Cuthbert's could benefit from a similar approach, one which
emphasizes participation by all members of their family. In a
family service children play an active part by reading the lesson,
helping with the offering, and (as they grow older) playing in the
orchestra, praying the prayers with the rest of their family, or
taking part in a dance, mime, or short drama. The messages are
simple and always involve visual aids of one form or another,
which holds the attention of all but the youngest children. Usually the messages get through to the parents as well, often with
much greater clarity and force than most conventional sermons!
Occasionally our service would be noisy because of the large
number of small children, but we always had an area where the
smallest ones could be taken at any time, so that others could
more easily concentrate in this family act of worship.

The philosophy behind the family service is important. While
the Sunday school aims to reach parents through children
(though in practice this very seldom happens, with many of the
children falling away from the church during their teenage
years), the family service aims to reach children through parents. Thus, although many aspects of it are planned with the
children in mind, we have always found this service to be one of
the best ways of winning parents for Christ. Then, once the
parents become Christians, they have much more potential for
helping their children through that rebellious and questioning

teenage phase. The family service helps bring whole families to Christ. In addition, this service, in contrast to Sunday school, helps children feel welcomed as a vital part of the wider family of God's people.

As soon as the family services started at St. Cuthbert's, we saw encouraging growth. When the first new family joined us, the congregation was immediately doubled and we welcomed each new family with excitement and joy. In the seventeen years we served at York, the family service naturally developed in various ways, but it was always a marvelous family occasion, which appealed to people of almost any age and background. Countless visitors to the church, especially those from overseas, were clearly moved by the whole service and commented that they had never seen anything like it.

We began to see these various encouraging signs at St. Cuthbert's, but as with any church, growth and development was far from easy. Traditionally, at least within Anglican circles, most church goers regard the church as a club: it is there for the convenience of members whenever they want to go, but few are expected to be actively involved in it. Sadly most clergymen have perpetuated this distortion of the nature of the church. In the New Testament church, however, every person, as a member of the body of Christ, played an indispensable part. Following our own traditional Anglican heritage, Anne and I began our ministry at York by doing almost everything ourselves. We departed from that practice once for two marvelous weeks in the spring of 1966 when many people joined together in decorating the whole church. It was like a mission to the congregation: it brought us much closer together. Apart from that, though, Anne and I carried most of the burden of ministry and gave all our time and energy trying to build a firm foundation for the future.

The congregation soon started to grow. After about six months the local press cautiously commented that "there was a reasonable chance that St. Cuthbert's would continue, according to a member of the Archbishop of York's Commission on Redundant Churches." Replying to this I said in my newsletter,

"We praise God that if the redundancy commission came to our church on some Sunday nights, they would be hard pressed to find a seat."

Once we were picketed by some York University students who were protesting the waste of these empty, redundant church buildings. These students were a little surprised when they saw streams of families coming into St. Cuthbert's, and when we invited the picketers to join us for the service we had to find extra chairs for them since all the others were occupied!

In January 1966 another major sphere of work began to open up for me: I lead my first university mission. This initial one was at Reading, where for twenty-five years successive student committees had discussed the possibility of sponsoring a mission. I assumed that, after discovering all the well-known speakers were booked up, the committee had stumbled on me. I found the student team as inexperienced and nervous as I was, and I could see at the pre-mission retreat that we needed something special from God if the mission were to make any impact at all. At that retreat I spoke on the nature of faith and the vital importance of being filled with the Holy Spirit if we were to be effective as witnesses to Christ. Then I asked all team members to go back to their rooms for the next half hour and seek the Spirit's power in their own lives. During that half hour God met with many of the students in a gentle but unmistakable way, and because of this they went into the mission full of boldness and faith.

There were only fifty students in the Christian Union, but with daring faith they put out 120 chairs for the mission's first meeting. Three hundred people turned up, and twelve gave their lives to Christ that night. For six nights students responded, and by the end of the time at least sixty had found Christ, most of them standing firm as Christians in the months and years ahead. Proportionately it was probably the most fruitful of the seventy to eighty university missions I have had the privilege of leading.

In personal terms, however, the cost of those developments in ministry proved considerable. During our first few months in York, Anne suffered a long and deep depression, once again withdrawing into herself and often sleeping for twelve hours or more each night. Whatever the basic reasons for this depression (exhaustion doubtless being one of them), it was only through a time of prayer and ministry by Michael and Jeanne Harper and others that the depression was lifted and Anne was again free.

I, too, had problems. Shortly before moving to York I had wonderfully received a temporary healing from asthma. Anne and I were at a gathering of friends at Gillingham where a remarkable person named Edgar Trout was ministering. Although some of his work was unorthodox, the power of God was manifestly with him, and this gathering unexpectedly turned into a whole night of prayer. I was coughing away as usual, so Edgar decided to anoint me with oil and he asked everyone to pray for me. They prayed and then started to praise God that he had answered their prayer for healing. It's all very fine for them, I remember thinking; they were having a great time of praise, but I was still coughing miserably. At about eight in the morning Anne and I tumbled into bed for a couple of hours feeling a little discouraged by the night's work, but when I woke up and got dressed I suddenly realized that I was no longer coughing. I could walk down the street, even run up the stairs, without coughing! Thus healed, I was able to enter into all the strenuous work at York without the affliction of asthma.

However, after the first nine months of demanding physical, mental, and spiritual work, the asthma started to return. Our fatigue and our individual problems made this an extraordinarily difficult time for each of us. In addition the strain of getting the work going in York contributed much tension to our relationship together. We both thought and reacted in such different ways that we couldn't really understand each other.

Into that stressful atmosphere our first child, Fiona, was born on August 10, 1966. My attitude at the time towards family life and its relation to church work was typified by my visit to the hospital after Fiona's birth. It was a brief visit when, hoping I was saying and doing all the right things, I prayed a short prayer of thanksgiving, patted Fiona gently on the head, gave Anne a little kiss, and rushed off to lead our parish fellowship. "First things first" had always been my unspoken motto; and for me, at that time and for many years to come, the work of the church came unquestionably before my responsibilities to my family. Since I hardly knew my father before he died, I understood little about fatherhood, and I fear that I have frequently been a poor husband and a worse father. Fiona, of course, brought us a tremendous amount of joy, but with her arrival came seemingly endless broken nights. This brought Anne to exhaustion once again, in turn increased my asthma, and (as I saw it) the rapidly growing work of the church was hindered. I had much to learn about God's priorities in life. I could have gained much from the apostle Paul who wrote that the quality of a man's relationship at home is a major factor in his qualification for Christian ministry.

A major crisis came for me in January 1967 when I went to Switzerland, without Anne and Fiona, to speak at the winter sports retreat organized by the Officers' Christian Union. In many ways it was a wonderful time when we saw God powerfully at work in people's lives. But my asthma became increasingly severe, possibly aggravated by the high altitude, and after two or three hopeless nights of sleeplessness, a decision was made to send me home a few days early. When I saw Anne at the train station, I noticed her look of anxiety and gave her a weak smile but scarcely had the breath to wheeze Hello. She had to push me wheezing and coughing along the platform on a porter's trolley.

Like a madman, as I see it now, I was off the next month to lead another university mission, this time in Trinity College, Dublin. Once again, I had to leave two days early due to severe asthma, and I realized something had to be done. Reluctantly I cancelled another university mission which I had been scheduled to lead in Durham ten days later.

My condition became so serious that Anne sent for our doctor in the early hours of the morning. I had been struggling for breath, and was so disoriented from lack of oxygen I apparently asked Anne if she was my optician! What I thought I was doing in bed with my optician I cannot begin to imagine. Our doctor arrived and gave me an injection, but it had no effect whatsoever. I was still gasping for breath. He gave me another injection which eased the situation a little, and he came back first thing in the morning with a consulting physician. The consultant explained that normally he would send me to the hospital immediately, but since Anne was a nurse he was prepared to risk sending us, with Fiona of course, away from York for three months' convalescence.

As I think about it now, I suppose I had a partial breakdown. At the time, although I felt relieved to be away from all responsibilities for a time (I couldn't think straight about anything), I felt utterly crushed by the apparent implications of my failure at a time when we could see God working powerfully. The work in York was just beginning to be really exciting. St. Cuthbert's Church had been packed out for several Sundays, and we needed to increase seating in the church. The Thursday Fellowship had also grown fast, and we were relaying the Bible study to several rooms in the rectory because so many people wanted to come. The universities, too, had unexpectedly opened up, and God was apparently using me for effective evangelism among students. My first book, one on youth work called *Towards Tomorrow's Church*, had recently been published and was well received. Everything seemed on the point of blossoming.

As I went away from it all for those three months, depression initially set in. I genuinely thought I would never preach again, never return to the work in York, never lead another mission, never write another book, and never really cope as husband and father. I felt a complete and total failure in virtually every area of my life. I had come to the end of myself. My natural strength had failed. Perhaps I had come to love the Lord's work more than the Lord himself. Whatever the spiritual reasons for that painful period, I had to hand back everything I knew to the Lord, and humbly, with empty hands, ask for his mercy, healing, and grace. The future was totally uncertain, and all I could hope for was the Lord himself. The only thing I could do during those three months was spend the time with Anne and Fiona. And that was the best thing I could have done.

9

St. Cuthbert's—
A Joyful
Expansion

"YOUR ABSENCE HAS BEEN SUCH A BLESSING TO US!" was the greeting we received on our return to York. It was good to know that we were not indispensable, and we took that delightfully ambiguous remark as a sign that God had by that time established his work in York, at least at a foundational level. Other members of the body had taken on the responsibilities we left behind and they had grown spiritually as a result.

The three months away from York had also been a time of considerable blessing to our own family. In spite of all the difficulties and tensions Anne and I had known, we still loved each other very much, which is probably why the tensions had been so traumatic. Our time off together, doing nothing except enjoying each other's company and taking constant delight in Fiona, reinforced our love, and in the peacefulness of those weeks my asthma subsided. By the end of our convalescence I was able to think about our ministry without always creating a spasm, and I realized after this period of humbling and chastening that my work for the Lord had not yet come to an end. In York, in fact, things had just begun.

During 1966 I had preached often about the person and work of the Holy Spirit, and I had spoken simply about the spiritual renewal that God was bringing all over the world. Since then a growing number within our congregation were not only finding a personal relationship with Christ, but they were also consciously being filled with the Spirit. Some were speaking in tongues, usually in private for their own personal prayer but occasionally in public during church prayer meetings, with interpretation following each time.

Some were also beginning to prophesy as they shared what they felt God was saying to us. We saw immediately how edifying this gift can be in the life of a congregation; it was never a substitute for the regular teaching from the Scriptures, but God at times used a simple message in prophecy to touch the hearts of his people in a remarkably personal way. We could see why the apostle Paul wrote so positively about this gift in 1 Corinthians 14.

We discovered the value of prophecy in evangelism too. A non-Christian student came to our church one evening, brought by her Christian friend. The student was embarrassed to discover she had come to a communion service. Feeling increasingly out of place in that atmosphere of joyful corporate worship, she walked out of the service halfway through. Later, however, she realized that she had left her scarf behind, so she returned when she thought the service would be over. Since we had finished administering the bread and the wine, the girl went up to the front pew to get her scarf. At that moment there was silence, followed by the flow of continuous praise, and then two members of the congregation brought words of prophecy they believed they had received from God. The student wrote to me the next day: "I heard my actual thoughts in the second prophecy—something I have never heard before. I heard God actually telling me, in a church with hundreds of other people present, not to run as I had done so often before...I felt and experienced God's presence—something terrifying yet wonderful." There and then she had surrendered her life to Christ.

The apostle Paul once wrote: "If all prophesy, and an unbeliever or outsider enters . . . the secrets of his heart are disclosed; and so, falling on his face, he will worship God and declare that God is really among you" (1 Cor. 14:24-25). This is exactly what happened with the visiting student. In hundreds of instances at St. Cuthbert's, God spoke directly to both Christians and non-Christians, with positive results affecting people's lives and drawing them closer to Christ.

During these years we also prayed much for individuals' healing: some were healed, and some were not. The whole ministry of healing often left us puzzled and confused, having to bow before the sovereign purposes of God. Yet when prayer for healing was sensitively handled, there was always blessing of one kind or another. We discovered also the value of the gifts of knowledge and wisdom. Sometimes God gave us by his Spirit an insight into the hidden needs of a person who obviously needed God's help, and we were able to get to the heart of the problem quite quickly. We are joyful that from these early years on there was never once a split in the congregation over this issue of spiritual gifts.

Many other gifts were developing in our group. I was particularly encouraged to see spontaneous gifts of evangelism emerging. People who had found the reality of God in their lives talked naturally to their friends about Christ. Some people brought friends to the guest services which we held about six times a year, when we would try to explain, as simply as we could, how anyone could find Christ. Many did find him. At the first service, only one young schoolgirl responded. After the service she courageously pushed her way through the stream of the congregation leaving the church. This York girl, Pauline Hornby, became a faithful and much-loved member of our congregation and later joined my full-time traveling team and worked with us for four years, before marrying our assistant organist Andrew Shepherd. At each subsequent guest service we saw a number of people, from three at the least to eighty at the most, outwardly profess faith in Christ, and doubtless there were many more we did not know about at the time. Consequently these guest services became well-known and popular, and soon an overflow of people regularly had to be channeled to a nearly hall where the service was relayed because St. Cuthbert's was packed to the doors and could hold no more. Later, as the numbers steadily increased, a regular closed circuit television system was installed for use during all the evening services, and the family services had a "repeat performance" each Sunday morning.

With good New Testament precedent, we had numerous house-meetings also. We realized that a new Christian has many friends, neighbors, and colleagues who are not true believers, so that he is in an ideal situation for sharing his faith with them. We found that these friends were interested in hearing more about this faith, and were quite willing to come to the informal atmosphere of a home where a speaker would give a short talk, often followed by a lively discussion. It was a marvelous, natural sphere for evangelism, and at almost every one of the many house-meetings held for this purpose we saw at least one person become a Christian. We felt much the same as St. Luke when he wrote about Samaria 2,000 years ago. "There was much joy in that city." For St. Cuthbert's, it was a time of spontaneous and joyful expansion.

The vision some had of our church becoming a resource center for students was also being fulfilled. Large numbers of students came to us from York University, St. John's College of Education, and other nearby colleges, and over the years a great many of these students came to Christ or were strengthened in their faith as a result. We also had a simple hospitality scheme, linking up students with families in our congregation whenever possible. Many deep friendships were formed in this way, and students loved getting away from campus life every now and then to spend time, often a Sunday, in the midst of ordinary family life. As the work grew we were able to designate one or more full-time members of our church staff to be available for counseling students. Naturally we also worked closely with the university chaplains whenever we could. We saw ourselves in a serving, supporting role, in no way providing a substitute for Christian fellowship and witness on the campus itself (if students are not committed to evangelizing students, however tough that might be at times, no one else will be). We believed strongly that a local church can help student Christians feel a part of the wider church. Indeed, we specifically aimed to help students prepare for the transition from their rather specialized Christian activities at college to membership in local churches afterwards. Through our ordinary Sunday services we could give students an experience of worship and of the body of Christ which they could never have known to the same degree on the campus itself. Many of the students benefited from the regular preaching they heard, and significantly there were comparatively few tensions over "charismatic" issues in York University, for example, compared with the problems in some other universities. Today I find it a constant joy to meet active Christians in many walks of life— not a few on the mission field or in the ordained ministry—who first became Christians during their student days in York, at least partly as a result of what they had experienced at our church.

The heart of our congregation was growing in depth and maturity, although we were still a very young church. About 140 people were regularly attending the Parish Fellowship each Thursday, filling six rooms to capacity in the rectory, with the Bible study relayed through a sound system to the rooms, and then a time of prayer within each room. This was an encouraging sign of growth in our congregation, but it put some strain on Anne and me. Since every midweek meeting in the church had to take place in the rectory (there was no other place available), Anne had to put up with a great deal, especially when Fiona was awakened by the constant coming and going, with bells ringing and doors slamming. Somehow we managed it, but often at the cost of depression for Anne, asthma for me, and tensions between us.

Requests for me to take outside speaking engagements began increasing rapidly after our first years at York. During the ensuing years I led missions at Cambridge, Oxford, Durham, Southampton, Keele, Sussex, Manchester, Birmingham, Aston, Bangor, Bristol, Leicester, Liverpool, Nottingham, Sheffield, and various other places, including several universities overseas. Most of these missions proved extraordinarily fruitful, with many hundreds of students finding Christ as a result. Letters kept pouring in. "I have never known such utter joy and quietness of mind," said one research student. "It is like living in a world which suddenly has an extra dimension." Another wrote: "I'll never be able to express my gratitude to Christ for the way he has become so real and living." Today I find it a great joy when I meet someone who professed conversion years ago at one of those missions and who is now actively serving Christ in some part of the world.

My frequent traveling, however, was a trial for Anne in those years. Although she knew that God was in it all, and to that extent accepted it, each time I went away she experienced deep within a sense of rejection or abandonment. This produced frequent tensions between us for two or three days prior to my departure, so much that I would often cry in desperation to God on my way to some university, "O Lord, I'm not sure how much more either Anne or I can take. If you really want me to do this work you will have to give us more grace."

Obviously I'm not suggesting that during those early years we knew nothing but pain and tears in our marriage. Our love for one another was always with us, in spite of many stormy scenes, and we had some hilarious moments as well. With so many people coming to the rectory each week, we found it difficult having only one lavatory, especially because it was up a flight of stairs. A friend of mine, who was an Army officer stationed at Catterick, said that his soldiers were doing nothing much, and so he could volunteer a work party to build us another lavatory on the first floor. After considerable difficulty they found the necessary plans showing the position of the water pipes and drains. The soldiers then dug through the thick clay soil to form a huge trench which gradually wound its way around our home. Winter set in and, with the backdoor frequently left open as soldiers went back and forth for cups of tea and visits to the lavatory, the rectory became an icebox. Then, when the trench was completely finished, all the troops were suddenly posted overseas, and we were left with an impressive moat around our house—a moat which rapidly filled with water and ice. (One night an unfortunate tramp actually fell into the moat and was covered with wet clay which he subsequently brought into our house.) With all the pressures of work, asthma, and general inefficiency, I am afraid it was months before I filled the trench in. Then we waited for almost 10 years before our second lavatory was actually installed.

Even when I was not away, Anne was quite often lonely. With me leading all the church services and meetings she was left alone with Fiona, missing the fellowship that others were enjoying. Moreover, mainly because of the domestic upheaval that follows the birth of a child, Anne was no longer reading her Bible and praying as she used to—at least not in the regular, disciplined way which had been her pattern in the past, and which was still very much my own. This made me quite anxious. Nevertheless, it was during this period of considerable loneliness and pain that Anne learned to listen to the Lord, to hear him speak to her. She discovered how to meditate on a word, a phrase, a verse, or an aspect of God's character. She found a new way of communicating with the Lord which was not dependent on the "regular quiet time" of her evangelical heritage. At times she would read her Bible for hours, but at other times her Bible remained closed for days or even weeks. But during this period she began to develop the prophetic ministry that God has especially used to touch the lives of so many people. The irritating thing for me was that, despite Anne's haphazard devotional life and my dogged discipline, Anne often seemed much more in touch with Christ than I was! Reluctantly I had to admit (and later to rejoice) that most of the best developments in York over the years came first through Anne's prophetic vision. I had to work out the ideas in my own terms, giving the church the necessary biblical teaching for each and then leading the people in the appropriate direction. Invariably, though, it was a direction that Anne had already seen several months, if not years, before.

The birth of our second child, Guy, happened in April 1969 in rather unusual circumstances. We probably got our dates wrong, but according to my diary the child should have been born by April 8. Therefore I readily accepted the invitation from a good friend of mine, Dick Lucas, to preach at three lunch hour services, on April 15, 22, and 29. By then Anne and the new baby should have been safely back at home. I was particularly keen to revisit St. Helen's Church in Bishopsgate, London, where Dick Lucas was Rector, because of the amazing work among city businessmen that God had developed through him. (Even now, after I have visited a good many cities in many parts of the world, I have never seen a comparable work among businessmen which has been so thorough and effective. It is truly a remarkable demonstration of the power of God through straightforward proclamation of his word in the Bible.)

Our baby did not arrive by April 8, and April 15 and 22 came and went, but still no baby was born. Early in the morning of April 29 it all started to happen. I rang for the midwife, and then dashed for the station to catch the London train since I had to preach my third lunch hour sermon at St. Helen's that day (my priorities still needed a drastic overhaul!). When I arrived at St. Helen's I rang the maternity hospital. "Put the phone down at once!" snapped the nurse at the other end. "The baby's coming right now!" Five minutes before the service was due to start I nervously dialed again. This time the nurse said, "You have a son, and both are doing fine!"

The title of my sermon had been printed some weeks before; it was "The New Birth." Nonchalantly I said from the pulpit, almost as an aside, "Ten minutes ago a son was born to me in York." I was later told that the few women present (the church is always packed out with men) ceased to listen to another word, their minds captivated by the thought of that newborn baby. However, I could not resist the evangelistic challenge that the event provided. "My wife was three weeks overdue," I said, not entirely sure of my medical knowledge. "Had it gone on much longer, it would have been dangerous for her. Spiritually speaking, some of you are not just three weeks overdue. You are thirty to forty years overdue. If you go on much longer this way it may be dangerous for you. Jesus said that you *must* be born again." The effect was quite dramatic.

We were overjoyed with Guy's birth and praised God for the gift of a son as well as a daughter. But once again we experienced broken nights for at least nine months with few exceptions, leading to more exhaustion, more asthma, more tensions, and further interruptions to the work. Yet through it all God continued to bless the church in York and the missions in universities.

Over and over since these early years I have been faced with the mysterious and inescapable link between suffering and blessing. The apostle Paul knew much about this, and he learned to be content with weaknesses, insults, hardships, persecutions, and calamities for he could say, "when I am weak, then I am strong" (2 Cor. 12:10). When he was weak the power of Christ rested especially upon him. Indeed he realized that God had actually given him a "thorn in the flesh." No one knows what this was, but most commentators believe that it was some physical handicap. God used it to keep him weak enough to receive grace for usefulness. God promised him sufficient grace, and power "made perfect in weakness" (2 Cor. 12:9). I came to view my asthma as a "thorn in the flesh." Like Paul, I asked for it to be removed; but through this weakness and other suffering we experienced, I found God's grace sufficient and his presence always evident. Our story is not one of human achievement, human wisdom, or human greatness; our church in York bears testimony to divine grace given during a continuing experience of human weakness, physical and spiritual, out of which came the joy of new life.

It is sometimes said that whereas God loves us just as we are, he loves us too much to leave us as we are. J. B. Phillips gave an accurate description of many of us when he titled one of his books *Your God Is Too Small.* We have a much too narrow vision of God. After Guy's birth I discovered that God wanted to expand my vision of him in ways that brought me a sunshine of surprises.

10

Widening Vision

A SIGNIFICANT MILESTONE IN MY LIFE came in 1971 when I participated in an international conference for spiritual renewal organized by the Fountain Trust at Guildford. Our friends Michael and Jeanne Harper had courageously sought to encourage renewal within the church, in spite of considerable misunderstanding and opposition, and Anne and I had already benefited from a number of Fountain Trust conferences they had promoted. The conference at Guildford, based at Surrey University, proved particularly challenging because it was the first time that I found myself a speaker on the same platform with Roman Catholic speakers.

Since my conversion, I had come to think that the Roman Catholic Church was an apostate church: it effectively denied the great Reformation doctrine of "justification by faith" through its insistence on many religious observances as necessary requirements for salvation; it exalted the Virgin Mary at times, it seemed, even above Christ himself; it taught that the bread and wine at the Mass mystically became the body and blood of Christ; it gave the Pope and Roman dogma an authority equal to that of the New Testament; it undermined the truths of salvation by its teaching about purgatory and by its prayers for the dead. In other words, it preached "another gospel," and the apostle Paul once wrote that anyone doing such a thing would be cursed by God! For me, the Roman Catholic Church was virtually synonymous with the Anti-Christ: a massive and powerful organization that had all of the form of the Christian religion but was in fact a Satanic counterfeit of the real thing. My "anti-Rome" position was almost akin to the most extreme Protestants in Northern Ireland, although I was less vocal about it. Nevertheless I was totally convinced of the truth of my own convictions, although I confess that rarely did I actually talk to Roman Catholics, and still less did I attempt to listen to what they were saying.

Once or twice in Cambridge I discussed the matter with Dr. Basil Atkinson, whose own attitude towards Catholics was even more colorful than my own. There was always a delightful eccentricity about Basil which could shock those who did not know him at all; but anyone who knew him realized how much he loved the Lord and how much he loved all those who knew Jesus personally, as he manifestly did. Therefore, in spite of his strongly anti-Roman background, Basil once asked me if I thought it were possible for Roman Catholic nuns to be saved. "Why do you ask?" I replied. "Because I have just met two nuns who seemed to be radiant for Jesus," he answered. "It seemed impossible, and yet it was true!" After that day I too met quite a number of Catholic nuns, priests, and laypeople who gave me the same impression, and I had to do some theological gymnastics to cope with it. However, these were still my own private thoughts, and I had not yet made any public comment about them.

The conference at Guildford was quite another matter. How could I share the same platform with leaders from an apostate church? By so doing, wasn't I compromising the truths for which many of the Reformers had died? As I took the risk and cautiously engaged in conversation with some of the Catholics present who were theologically articulate, two facts came home to me. First, they showed me much more love and acceptance than I was able to show them. Second, when we got down to the basic issues—justification by faith, the finished work of Christ on the cross, the place of the Virgin Mary, the doctrine of the Mass, and the supreme authority of Scripture—to my astonishment, some of the problems I had seen were purely a matter of semantics (using words in different ways). The more I listened the more I was impressed by the biblical position they held. We did not totally agree about everything; but concerning many essential elements of the gospel there seemed little, if any, difference. I realized that some of their thinking was directly the result of the Spirit's renewing work in their own minds and hearts (the Holy Spirit is always the Spirit of truth), and I felt that some of the views of those present at this conference were not typical of official Catholic teaching, at least not before Vatican II (1963-65). How then, I wondered, could these leaders remain in the Roman Catholic Church and not demonstrate their new life in Christ by coming out of it?

As I thought and prayed about this, I felt that God was saying: "David, I'm not first and foremost concerned about your convictions, but I am concerned about your attitudes. And your attitudes towards those with whom you do not agree are all wrong. First get your attitudes right, and then we can talk about your convictions." I wanted to protest because on various important issues I was so sure that I was right and that others (not only Roman Catholics) were wrong. But those words of Paul hit me very powerfully: "And if...I understand...all knowledge...but have not love, I am nothing" (1 Cor. 13:2). I began to repent deeply of my negative, critical attitudes. I confessed my spiritual arrogance. I acknowledged my lack of love towards others, especially professing Christians with whom I did not agree.

The battle was not won overnight, far from it. But as I continued to ask the Spirit of God to change my negative attitudes, I found that he was giving me an altogether new love towards many non-evangelicals, even Roman Catholics. What was more, as my attitudes changed I began to listen to people, some of them for the first time. I began to hear what they really believed, not what I thought they believed. I discovered vast numbers of true brothers and sisters in Christ whom I never knew existed. I started trying to believe the best about people instead of always fearing the worst. I learned that God had many things to teach me, often through people from traditions different than my own. I began to see how rich and varied is the worldwide body of Christ, and I praised God for releasing me from the spiritual blinders that I had worn for so long. I saw that the sovereignty of God, working in different ways among different people, was more wonderful than I had ever previously understood. Even passages of Scripture spoke to me in new ways as I tried to fathom a little bit more of the "depth of the riches and wisdom and knowledge of God."

All these new impressions were confirmed many times over in the ensuing years, and I often had remarkable times of fellowship with all sorts of people I would never have associated with in previous times. One unforgettable experience was the Third National Conference on Charismatic Renewal in Ireland, at the Royal Dublin Society Showground in September 1976. I went as the opening speaker, and was amazed to find 6,000 present, of whom 5,000 were Roman Catholic (including many hundreds of nuns and priests) and 1,000 were Protestant. It was an incredible conference, and I was especially impressed by the God-centered, Christ-centered nature of it all. Every meeting began with a prolonged time of worship; it seemed that the participants were not willing to listen to any speaker until they had first fixed their minds and hearts on God himself. It was obviously the Lord whom they wanted to hear, not just some ordinary speaker! Equally obvious was their hunger for God's Word: they loved to hear the Scriptures expounded. They were also profoundly aware of the difference between religion and the "real thing." It was astonishing for me to hear Roman Catholic priests saying from the platform to this vast crowd: "It is not enough being born as a Catholic; you need to be born again by the Spirit of God. It is not enough to come to Mass each week; you need to know Jesus Christ as your personal Lord and Saviour." It was almost like a Billy Graham crusade!

Most moving of all was the Service of Reconciliation on Saturday night. Led by a small group of Protestant and Catholic leaders, we came to see from a good exposition of Ephesians chapter two that the cause of our divisions in home, church, and society, is always sin in the heart of man. Through simple drama enacted in front of a huge empty cross, we saw that the only place for reconciliation is at the foot of the Cross. We each had come to the Cross not as a Protestant or a Roman Catholic, but as a sinner. There, when we put our trust in the one Savior who died for our sins once for all, God had accepted each one of us as "my son," or "my daughter." Because of this we should call one another, "my brother" or "my sister."

After the drama, we were all invited to go to anyone within that huge hall, to ask for forgiveness for anything we had said or done in the past that had grieved the Spirit of God. I was at once surrounded by a large crowd of nuns and priests asking for forgiveness from me, as a representative Protestant, for things that they had said and done that were not right; and of course I reciprocated. Then we embraced one another as brothers and sisters; experiencing at a deeper level than I had ever known before what it means to be "one body through the Cross." If we belonged to Christ, we belonged to one another also; and what God has joined together through the death of his own Son, man must never put asunder.

The next day, in obedience to our respective traditions, we separated for the Catholic Mass and the Protestant Eucharist. Most of us were in tears for much of the service because we felt deep within our hearts (I had never experienced this before) the grief that Christ must feel over his torn, lacerated, and divided body here on earth—a body split into more than 20,000 registered Christian denominations alone, not to mention the tensions and divisions within any given denomination or local church. Ever since that conference I have sensed a little bit of the pain that Christ must always feel when we separate from one another, when in effect we say to him, "You died to make us one, and we don't care!"

After this conference in Ireland I began to speak more openly about the importance of our oneness in Christ, and the urgent need we have for reconciliation in the church if we want to have any credible ministry of reconciliation in the world. At the Nottingham Evangelical Anglican Conference (NEAC) in 1977 I spoke on the mission of the church from Luke chapter ten. One of my eleven points was the vital importance of unity, and *in that context* I went on to say that "in many ways the Reformation was one of the greatest tragedies that ever happened to the church." I then explained, "Martin Luther never wanted to split the church, simply to reform it. All of you no doubt glory in the biblical truths that were rediscovered at the Reformation (as I certainly do), but from the Reformation onwards the body of Christ in the world has been torn limb from limb into hundreds of separate pieces." When I called the Reformation one of the greatest tragedies in the church, there was an audible gasp in the conference hall. In the *context* in which it was said, it was a perfectly fair statement. If only the church in 1517 had been willing to accept the reformation that Martin Luther, himself a Roman Catholic monk, had tried to effect, we might never have divided into these thousands of little fragments.

That particular sentence of my message was inevitably a gift-horse for any journalist: "David Watson says that the Reformation was the greatest tragedy in the history of the church!" Taken out of its context it sounded worse than heresy to any warm-blooded Protestant. I had many stinging and condemning letters sent to me from some of my Reformed brethren, and I still receive an occasional one. Some will never forgive me for that remark, and would like to see it inscribed on my tombstone no doubt! Yet, having repented and continuing to repent of my own critical attitudes, I longed for a new spirit of repentance to come upon the church. I saw this as an absolute priority before any revival came: "If my people who are called by my name humble themselves, and pray and seek my face, and turn from their wicked way, then I will hear from heaven, and will forgive their sin and heal their land" (2 Chron. 7:14). For example, with all the bitterness which has perpetuated the violence in Northern Ireland for so many years, surely there can be no true healing of relationships until there is first a deep repentance for sin—not just the sin of violence, but even more the sin of bitterness which lies at the heart of these troubles. The same principle is true wherever we Christians are not loving one another as Christ has loved us, or welcoming one another as Christ has welcomed us, or forgiving one another as Christ has forgiven us. Until we sort out our relationships with one another, our relationship with God is not right; and he waits for us to repent before he can renew us with his Spirit of love and truth.

When I was leading a festival of praise in St. Anne's Cathedral, Belfast, both Protestants and Roman Catholics were warmly invited, and a number of priests and nuns were present. Some rather militant Protestants picketed the service outside the main doors, and handed out tracts to everyone coming in. One of these tracts showed a lot of ants marching towards Rome. They apparently represented us, since we were Protest-ants who had left out the protest in what we were doing. We were therefore only "ants" heading stupidly in a Popish direction. It was a rather sick joke, but it was meant to be deadly serious. How much is the spirit of repentance needed among us all!

A further development in my vision of God and his work came in the summer of 1972 when Anne and I left Fiona and Guy with Anne's parents in Cheshire and went for several weeks to North America, on an exchange-of-preaching scheme organized by the British Council of Churches. Among many fascinating experiences, we were particularly struck by the quality of worship that we experienced in an Episcopal church in Virginia. In many respects the service was nothing much to write home about: the musicians and singers were not unusually talented. But they had about them a gentle quality of intimate worship which refreshed us just as if we'd been given a cup of cold water in the desert. They were obviously singing not just *about* the Lord, but *to* the Lord, and their worship brought a sense of God's presence into the service in a quiet but most effective way.

That experience was followed shortly afterwards by a morning service at St. Margaret's Community Centre in Vancouver, where the pastor was Bob Birch. Bob was a man whom you might not look at twice on the street; there was nothing outwardly impressive about him. But his whole life was directed totally towards Christ, and he was one of the most prayerful and godly men I had ever met. However, what struck us more than the pastor was the church itself. We had never been anywhere before where we felt so completely overwhelmed by love. As I looked around that packed-out church—people were sitting everywhere—I noticed an amazing mixture of ages and backgrounds. All the normal social and cultural barriers were broken down by the love of Christ. Barefoot students in jeans were sitting next to bank managers in pin-stripe suits. And the worship in the church was simply glorious. Everyone seemed totally absorbed in the act of loving Christ through praise and prayer. You could see from their faces that the vast majority were profoundly aware of his living presence in our midst, and again they were singing *to* the Lord. The service, although non-liturgical, was ordered and dignified; at the same time there was a spontaneity and freedom about it so that words of prophecy and singing in tongues seemed perfectly natural and in no way contrived.

The whole hour was broadcast every Sunday over local radio, and calls came in all the time from needy people in different parts of Vancouver. Those calls for help would be answered immediately and without any fuss by teams sent out from the congregation, so that the service had an immediacy and relevance about it that was unmistakable. I preached for about 20 minutes and, after another hymn, the radio service came to an end. I had not realized that the congregation in the church would go on for another hour or so, with more free worship, praise, prayer, and the exercise of spiritual gifts, all of which proved intensely edifying. Then I discovered that I was expected to preach again! Quickly I put a few thoughts together from Ephesians 5, and rather clumsily preached my second sermon. Nevertheless several people came forward for counseling. After the final hymn and benediction a woman sang exquisitely in a tongue, both language and music given to her by the Holy

Spirit. Then she sang, equally exquisitely, the interpretation of
the tongue. What I found especially moving and humbling
about this was that, in her short song in the Spirit, the woman
summed up perfectly what I had been struggling to say in my
second twenty-minute sermon! I learned later that the woman
normally had quite an unimpressive voice; but when it was con-
trolled by the Spirit it certainly had a breath of heaven about it.
As Anne and I left the church that day we felt that if God was
anywhere on the face of this earth, he surely was in that service.

Through those fleeting experience in Virginia and Vancouver, God increased my vision to include an altogether new
understanding of worship, and he gave me a fresh glimpse of the
body of Christ in action. At the time of our trip, I was beginning
to think that we had "arrived" at St. Cuthbert's, because the
work had been developing so rapidly. After these experiences
overseas I knew that we had so much more to learn, and I was
thrilled with the prospect of new horizons opening up. An official report on our church commented: "Members of the congregation noticed a much more liberated minister when he
returned to St. Cuthbert's, and there was greater freedom, joy,
and spontaneity in worship...Praise became the dominant
note." It was not that we lessened our biblical teaching—far
from it. However we gave a lot of positive teaching about the
primacy and nature of worship.

In my travels I had seen, almost as if for the first time, the rich
variety of worship mentioned in the psalms. I had realized, too,
how straightjacketed we had become with our stilted, formal
services, or with our hearty evangelical hymns. How little we
understood about adoration in worship! How stiff we were in
any physical expression! In the Anglican church we were used to
kneeling as a posture symbolizing reverence and humility. But
how inhibited we were when it came to clapping, raising hands,
or dancing. Even as a "much liberated minister" I was still quite
a long way from all that. At the Guildford Conference Michael
Harper had encouraged us to lift up our hands in praise to the
Lord, but inwardly I had replied, "Not on your life!" I was
standing next to the Dean of the Cathedral and I told myself that

I would not raise my hands so as not to embarrass him; but it was really me who was irritated by this un-English display of religious fervor. Interestingly, hardly anyone else at the conference seemed to have my problem!

All this fresh stimulus was preparing our congregation for a major step forward in God's work among us. Numerically, by 1971-1972 we had reached saturation point at St. Cuthbert's. We packed over 200 in our small building, sometimes even more. Anyone who wished to get a seat for the evening service had to come at least forty-five minutes early; after that they had to go to one of two large rooms in another building fifty yards away where the service was relayed on closed-circuit television. For guest services we had to extend our facilities even further by arranging for a sound relay to a third building. It was marvelous seeing the crowds pouring in and out, but we were also hearing of some who no longer came because there simply was not enough room. We prayed much for guidance.

11

Our Move to
St. Michael-le-Belfrey

As we prayed about the space problem at St. Cuthbert's, a letter arrived one morning from a friend asking why on earth the diocese had not offered us St. Michael-le-Belfrey Church, just opposite York Minster. St. Michael's was almost three times the size of St. Cuthbert's. It was almost empty and plans for declaring it redundant had been completed. The documents were just waiting for the archbishop's signature. Rather similar to St. Cuthbert's, St. Michael's was also likely to become a museum, this time housing artifacts for the Minster.

Two or three years before this I had tentatively approached various diocesan officials about the possibility of our moving into St. Michael's, but I had been given a polite but firm refusal. If the idea was right, the timing had been wrong. Then, after my friend's letter, through the excellent work of the archdeacon of York, the Venerable Leslie Stanbridge, backed strongly by Morris, the bishop of Selby, and Donald, the archbishop of York, a provisional experimental scheme of moving the congregation from St. Cuthbert's to St. Michael's was approved within two months, surely breaking all records in the Church of England!

On January 1, 1973 we moved our Sunday services from one building to the other. This was to prove much more significant than we could possibly have realized at the time.

One month before that, however, we saw another unusual development. I remember I was standing on the platform at York railway station when a good friend of mine, a member of our congregation, said, "David, have you ever thought of holding our guest services in York Minster?" The idea had never remotely crossed my mind; we were packed out at St. Cuthbert's, but ours was really a very small building and the minster is the biggest Gothic cathedral in the world. Even with our guest service congregation of about 700, we would be lost in the minster. Nevertheless, encouraged by my friend, I approached one or two of the minster canons to discover their reactions.

The minster had recently gone through extensive renovation costing about $4.5 million, during which crumbling foundations had been strengthened, a magnificent undercroft opened, the exterior cleaned, and the interior decorated. It was now a superb sight, probably in a finer state of glory than ever before in its long history. At the rededication service of the renovated minster the archbishop of York had said that he hoped the building would be not just a monument but the very gate of heaven to thousands who came within its walls.

The minster clergy were surprisingly positive about my unusual inquiry, and they agreed that we could organize an Advent guest service in the cathedral on December 3. They gave me every possible help in planning this. At times I was afraid that we had attempted an impossible task, and that at least half of the huge nave would be quite empty. However, the media got hold of this extraordinary idea of a tiny parish church holding its service in the vast minster, and there was a fair amount of free and unexpected publicity in the papers and on radio and television. The result was that the minster was not only full to its seating capacity, but extra chairs were brought in, and many people sat on kneelers on the floor. It turned out to be a wonderful service, and that night many gave their lives to Christ.

The minster clergy seemed just as delighted as we were; and thus encouraged by them, we began a series of minster services (about six a year), to which groups would come by bus from a wide area. Many clergy and ministers closed down their evening services in country areas, and brought their congregations along. It's hard to know quite why they came, but the services had a popular appeal because of the themes we chose and the way those themes were developed. We taught explicitly from the Bible, trying to relate its message to the obvious issues of the day, and we set the teaching in the context of joyful worship, led not only by the organ but also by a singing group with a variety of instruments. In later services our worship was often expressed in dance, and my sermons were illustrated by drama. We erected a large stage halfway down one side of the long central nave. Then we arranged all the chairs around the stage so we had much better visual contact with everyone in the congregation.

Jesus once described the kingdom of heaven in terms of a sumptuous marriage feast, something enormously attractive to hungry people: "Come, all is now ready!" The great Jewish festivals as well had been times of marvelous celebration, marked by color and music and singing and dancing, as the mighty acts of God were re-told. In this depressing age the Christian church is learning again how to celebrate. We realize we can not only talk about the magnificent banquet of the gospel but also invite people to experience it through the joyful and festive context in which the gospel is proclaimed. We can recapture some of the colorful drama of those superb festivals of the Jews, knowing that their hopes and expectations have been fulfilled in Christ. At York Minster as we attempted to set the jewel of Christ in the crown of celebration, we found that many wanted to join us. All those special minster services were occasions of much mutual encouragement, and through them many hundreds came into a personal relationship with Christ. The experiment exceeded all our expectations and also gave us an excellent relationship with the clergy of the minster, which was most important now that we had become immediate neighbors.

We had begun to see, too, that the timing of our move to St.

Michael-le-Belfrey was just right. Not only was the building saved at the last moment from being declared redundant (which in itself would have been a negative witness to the relevance of the Christian faith for today), but the style and setting of St. Michael's was utterly appropriate for the next phase of God's work among us. In St. Cuthbert's we were out on a limb, experimenting freely with services, largely doing our own thing (trying hard to be meaningful), but paying only lip service to the Anglican liturgy. In St. Michael-le-Belfrey, however, we were at the heart of a famous city, next to a famous minster, and under the gracious but eagle eye of a famous archbishop.

Once the costly job of cleaning, decorating, and re-wiring the building was finished, we gradually became aware of the new responsibilities that God had given us. York is a tourist city, attracting about two and a half million visitors from all over the world each year, and all of them, with hardly an exception, came to our very doorstep to visit the minster. Added to that, God's work among us at St. Michael's was beginning to be known throughout Great Britain and further afield, and we found an increasing number of visitors joining us for our Sunday services. When members of our own congregation were away on holiday in August, as many as eighty percent of the 700 present could be visitors.

We saw our responsibility in all this in two complementary ways. First, we realized that if the renewing work of the Spirit was of any significance at all, it must be worked out within the mainline denominations. In Ezekiel's vision of the valley of the dry bones, when the wind of the Spirit came, the bones were not blown away as dead and useless. God could have done that, and created new people in their places. In fact, however, the bones came together, they were clothed with flesh, and God breathed his life into them. I was (and still am) convinced that God's purpose is to renew the dry bones of existing Christian traditions, and we should not by-pass them in favor of something more immediately exciting. It always saddens me when I see Christians leave their denominations to join a new independent church; it is precisely in this way that all the 20,800 denominations in the world today came into being. Jesus weeps over our self-destructive divisions, which ironically only help to deny the gospel that we try to preach.

In St. Michael's, therefore, we became more consciously Anglican, even though my work was becoming increasingly ecumenical. If the renewal of the Spirit had no place in the Anglican tradition (or in any other mainline tradition), it was of no value at all. We adopted the new Anglican liturgies since these represented the liturgical renewal of various Christian traditions around the world. We did not want St. Michael's to have an identity all of its own. We were not out to build our own empire, with our own order of service different from everyone else's. We were a tiny part of the "one holy catholic and apostolic church" and we felt we must maintain a clear visible identity with that church. When the archbishop came, for example, we did not suddenly have to change our pattern of service; it was just the same format as anyone else might find visiting any Sunday in the year, with rare exceptions. We realized that only as we came clearly under the authority of the church could we be of any service to the church. In fact, the more we willingly and gladly submitted ourselves to those over us in the Lord, the more the blessing of God seemed to be upon us.

Second, we learned to discover "freedom within form." Once we had accepted the form of the Anglican liturgy as our basic identity (everyone has some identifiable form, even the most "independent" churches), we found plenty of freedom within that form. For example, we realized that in this latter part of the twentieth century we should not be tied only to the hymns and music of the eighteenth and nineteenth centuries. Some of those hymns are almost timeless, but many new songs and hymns are being written to express the life of the Spirit in today's church. Through the marvelous ministry of the Fisherfolk, a singing group gifted in leading people in worship, we learned the combination of dignity and joy, depth and simplicity, quality and gentleness, spiritual sensitivity and artistic skill. We found that through the gentleness of worship the Spirit of God can touch and heal inner wounds borne by countless people today, often the result of broken relationships. When members of our own congregation later began to write and compose songs, we found that the songs that had the special quality of tenderness about them usually were conceived out of suffering and tears.

It was in St. Michael's, too, that we learned much about the more visual expressions of worship and of the gospel. Most traditional church buildings make drama, mime, or dance virtually impossible. Narrow chancels, restricting choir pews, and massive pulpits eliminate all but the preacher and choir. We found these problems in St. Michael's, but a careful inspection of the choir pews (by me) revealed some woodworm. Admittedly there was not a lot of it, but enough to rip those pews out altogether, leaving a marvelous space between the front pews and the communion rails—a space that we later used to considerable advantage every Sunday. In addition, during a visit to Christchurch Cathedral in New Zealand, I was particularly impressed by a simple design for a large stage which could be erected or dismantled within a matter of minutes. The dean of Christchurch kindly gave me a copy of the design, and we built a similar one for ourselves. It was, and is, in constant use at St. Michael's and with it we began to learn about relevant communication for the world of today, still holding firm to the traditions of the church to which we belonged.

During this time of settling into St. Michael's, the small congregation that had kept the church from closing needed much grace to welcome the hundreds who came from St. Cuthbert's. It was not easy for them. In spite of being true to the basic Anglican liturgy, St. Cuthbert's style of music, worship, and most other things was clearly different. A few from the original congregation stayed, including Peter Gibson, the minster glazier, and a world expert on stained glass. Peter soon won everyone's affection by his wise diplomacy, his humble serving spirit, and his great sense of humor. But others found the crowds and changes too difficult and looked for a quieter home in the minster. This was sad, but quite understandable. Journalists occasionally tried to draw out from me unfavorable comments about the minster services which were obviously much more formal than our own. Always I resisted this and refused to say—or even think—that we were right and they were wrong. Their style of worship was no doubt just as valid, but it was primarily for more traditional Anglicans. We were attempting to make the same basic traditions live for those who had little or no church background, but who had become spiritually alive in Jesus Christ.

Over the years we had seen many individuals and families brought to Christ and filled with the Spirit. We were experiencing renewal and were anxious to see it spread. My short visit with Anne to North America, however, had given us an altogether new understanding of worship and of the body of Christ. I began to be aware that we had much more to learn in both these directions before we could share more widely anything significant about the renewal of the church. We realized that in many churches, some of the gifts needed for building up the body seem to be either not present at all, or not yet developed; besides, those who may be gifted in certain ways are usually far too busy to give more than a very limited part of their time to the work and mission of the church. We had to discover ways of releasing men and women for the work to which God might be calling them.

12
The Growth of Community

"I THINK WE OUGHT TO SHARE OUR HOME WITH OTHERS," Anne said to me one day.

"We've done that already," I replied defensively. "All sorts of people have stayed in our house for short and long periods. We've hardly been on our own since we moved to York."

"Yes, but they've only been lodgers, such as those university students, or close friends. There are so many others whose primary problem is loneliness, who need to belong to a family. Anyway, we have to learn to share our lives together if we're ever truly going to be the body of Christ."

I was slowly discovering that Anne had a visionary and prophetic ministry, although I usually questioned it very carefully. With some hesitation I agreed to open our home gradually to those who were willing to come not as lodgers, but as part of a community. Anne's vision was much wider than she initially revealed. She felt that a community of shared lives would deepen the sense of community throughout the whole church, even though the majority of our congregation would not adopt this lifestyle. We had the obvious model of the early church who had "all things in common." The strength and credibility of their witness lay largely in the quality of their corporate life together. "See how these Christians love one another!" was the cry of the pagan observer.

Anne also saw that extended households could considerably facilitate ministries within the church. The cry of most churches is lack of money and shortage of manpower (or personpower, to be non-sexist!). Most churches cannot get anywhere near the number of workers they need, and even if they could find the personnel, they could never pay for them. However, by sharing our homes and possessions, we could release both money and people for the work of the kingdom of God.

It was fascinating to see as the years progressed that both these visions which Anne saw so clearly were fulfilled beyond anything we had imagined possible when we took our first faltering steps toward them.

To begin with we had little concept about who should join our family. They just came. The first was a girl with a long history of mental instability, who had for many years frustrated the efforts of her doctors and psychiatrists. For almost two years she was a marvelous member of our household, opening up our closed lives toward others in need, welcoming everyone with great enthusiasm and cheerfulness, teaching Anne to cater for the large numbers who filled our house, and dealing swiftly and firmly with those who had just come off drugs but were secretly trying to pursue the habit (she took at least one girl down to the hospital to have her stomach pumped). As much as we loved her, however, we were unable to help her beyond a certain point, partly owing to her natural strength of personality; and very sadly I had to ask her to leave and return to her own home. I felt a terrible sense of failure which haunted me for months afterwards, especially when we heard indirectly that she was going through some rough times. It was an early and painful lesson that not all household living is "successful," and it helped us realize we had to clarify our aim: did God want us to concentrate on those who had special personal problems, or what?

Others came for a variety of reasons. Andrew Maries, a gifted musician who later became our musical director, originally brought his laundry over for Anne to do, at her suggestion, and stayed for a number of meals. At the time he was living a typical bachelor's existence, and before long it was a natural progression that he should join us. For several months I found that he irritated me beyond measure, and no doubt I did the same for him. Temperamentally we seemed such opposites, and everything he said and did drew out the worst in me. I could see that household living is not always easy partly because in the pressure of sharing our lives together we begin to see ourselves as we really are, not as we fondly imagine ourselves to be. Such lifesharing calls on us to remember constantly that the Lord is concerned not so much with the situation, however trying or irritating it may be, but with our reaction to that situation. After some months with Andrew I said, "Lord, I'm not sure I can stand having him in our house much longer. If you want him to stay here, you must do something about it." I'm not sure what God did about it, but I do know that Andrew soon became one of our closest friends and stayed in our household for seven years. We felt almost bereaved when he moved out of our home to marry Alicia, although in another sense we were thrilled to see the two of them come together. Alicia had been a member of our household for three years before moving out to become a district midwife, and we had all been extremely fond of her.

Another aim of the extended household was to develop the reality of brotherhood in the church so strongly that single people would not have to spend much of their time wishing and waiting to get married. We saw that in today's society there is such pressure on a single person to be married, or at least to enter into a sexual relationship with someone, that the disappointments and scars of broken relationships are to be seen everywhere. Jesus, however, called men and women into a new society where they could be first and foremost brothers and sisters in the family of God. Certainly marriage is a gift of God, and something to be held in honor by all; but Christ wants us to enjoy a depth of relationship with one another that is not always leading towards a sexual union. Many who enjoy community life find depths of commitment with other people that can release them from the trap of thinking only in terms of marriage or sex. However, within those deeply committed relationships of love and service, we were always delighted when two people eventually got married, especially when they had worked through some of the pressures and problems of a single life in today's permissive society.

We found it a joy to see people maturing during their time with us. Andrew is one example. As musical director he now shows a quality and sensitivity which he might not have had apart from all the blessings and traumas of community life. Through his musical leadership many discover in St. Michael's a gentleness in worship that speaks of joy through pain, something that they do not easily find in other places. I can see that just as God rubbed off some of my rough edges through my early abrasive encounters with Andrew (and others!), God may have used both the riches and tensions of household living to increase his work of grace in Andrew, whom he was preparing as a worship leader to encourage many churches throughout this country.

Others joined our household for shorter or longer periods of time—the shortest was about three months—and our roomy Victorian rectory usually had ten to twelve people living in it, our nuclear family being just four. For many years there was a lot of coming and going, and beds and other furniture were constantly being moved from one room to another. One girl was hardly off the drug scene, and she had to leave us before too long because she needed more specialized care than we could give her. However, our children grew especially fond of her during her short stay, and it was with immense sadness that we learned several years later that she had committed suicide. Another failure, to put it crudely. We had to learn humbly that we could not do everything, and that our ministry within the household had definite limitations. We also had to be willing for people to be with us only for a time, perhaps for quite a short time, and then to let them go peacefully out of our household to some other place. We found this quite difficult, and sadly when one or two people left, our relationship with them afterwards was strained, or even non-existent. This was not right, and we had to learn both how to welcome people and how to release them.

Along with the struggle and the disappointments we had many encouragements as we saw the healing power of God's love coming through a community of his people. Teresa's story is an example. "Will you go and see a girl who needs help?" asked a Roman Catholic Sister who had become a dear friend of ours. "Teresa comes from an impossible home situation, has absolutely no faith, and has just attempted suicide. She is in a mental hospital, yet she is a bright 16-year-old girl with quite a future. She simply needs a family."

I went with another household member to see Teresa, and it was clear to us immediately that she needed to get out of that hospital as soon as possible and find a home. We took her home with us. Her whole life needed sorting out, but most of all she needed to be loved. Within the growing sense of God's family in our house, Terri soon gave her life to Christ, went back to continue her studies at the Roman Catholic convent in York, and became a delightful member of our household. Naturally she had her difficulties. But it brought us immense joy to see her successfully passing her exams, going to Stirling University, getting married from our house (we were effectively her family), having a child, and more recently settling in South America as a healthy wife and mother with a strong Christian commitment. Anne had virtually become Terri's adopted mother as well as her sister in Christ, and those links remain strong to this day.

For the first two years, this new way of living seemed to threaten many in our church, and we felt distinct opposition. It may have been partly because our relationships within the household became unusually deep, as we related to one another as brothers and sister in Christ. Possibly others in the church were jealous of the special relationship that some had with "the rector and his wife." I suspect also that our opening of our home in this way was an inevitable challenge to those who naturally valued the privacy of their own family life. We had taken great care not to press this way of living on others, teaching that it was *one* valid way of expressing Christian community—not the only way, and not necessarily the best. I fully understood the sense of threat that many felt, however much we tried to avoid putting pressure on other families to follow suit, because I found this exercise of sharing all of life extremely difficult myself.

"An Englishman's home is his castle" is the old saying, and I was startled to find out how deep such a cultural trait could go. To begin with I resented others treating my furniture, my possessions, my money, my car, and sometimes even my clothes, as if they were their own. After our first four months, when I was still very unsure whether or not we were doing the right thing, I went to New Zealand for eight weeks. At the end of that time I naturally was longing to see Anne, Fiona, and Guy, but I was not so keen on having to see the rest of the household (three or four others at that time). On my return, I found a practical joke waiting for me. Knowing that I was every inch a typical Englishman who valued his privacy, the group had put up three cots in my study, and had strewn pajamas and clothes all over my little sanctuary! I was not amused. Indeed after a journey of thirty-six hours I was exhausted and disoriented, and the little joke threw me into a depression for a few days. Fortunately Betty Pulkingham and the Fisherfolk came to stay with us the day after I returned and Betty, with her wisdom and experience, told the household in no uncertain terms never to pull that prank again when I returned home from a tour. Apparently something similar had been done to Graham Pulkingham, then rector of the Church of the Redeemer, Houston, Texas, shortly after the Pulkingham's had adopted this community style of living. The results then were equally unfortunate.

Early in this venture we found that some clear structure was essential to keep everyone from just "doing their own thing." We knew that prayer must be the basis of our household, and virtually the only time we could meet together regularly was at 7:00 A.M., when we would spend thirty minutes sharing together from the Scriptures and praying for one another and for the needs of that day. It wasn't always easy to maintain this discipline, but we all recognized the importance of it and held each other to the commitment. Usually one member of the household would take notes as each person shared. Then he or she would summarize what it seemed that God was saying to us that day. As a by-product this practice encouraged us all to read our Bibles on our own so we would have something fresh to share each morning. We also had lists of household duties, with everyone rotating on dish duty and so forth. Beside that each person had an individual assignment, and mine was the simple task of carrying out the trash cans! We made quite clear the priorities of household living. First, everyone must support the ministry of the house, which in our case included several growing ministries at St. Michael's as well as my own wider work. Second, everyone must support the children and see them as young but vital members of the household. Third, everyone must support one another and express this by serving each other in practical and specific ways. Then, if they had any energy left, they could look after their own interests!

Although Anne and I exercised joint headship over the household, and to that extent were house parents, we worked hard on developing brother-sister relationships with all members, so that everyone had the freedom to "speak the truth in love." I sometimes found it difficult and humbling being rebuked by someone half my age; but the rebuke was usually justified, and I learned to take as well as give. Once a week, to begin with (less often later on) we had an evening household meeting when we would share together at greater length. We raised anything on our minds, even points of criticism or irritation, and prayed together, often ministering to one another at the same time. Occasionally these were very painful sessions when truths that were hard to face would be spelled out, ending perhaps in tears. Yet it was through these times that we learned a lot about ourselves, and the Spirit of God was able to heal areas of our lives that needed sorting out.

In spite of the threat that we posed to some members of our church, the obvious value of such a household became impressed on several families and individuals. After two years, six or seven other households emerged within the church, with families moving in together, single people joining a nuclear family, or widows, widowers, or single parents moving in to belong to a larger family. We spent much of our time trying to encourage and guide them, but some of them were not successful. Because of the many pitfalls in this way of living and the many principles we were having to learn the hard way, we increasingly discouraged enthusiastic couples in other places from following our example. In addition, although we did not always keep rigidly to this, we saw wisdom in inviting a person to join us for a probationary period of three to six months before he or she made a more definite commitment. During those months we would all try to sense whether or not the person was suitable for this particular way of life, which we knew was not for everyone.

The venture, which lasted for several years in York, was frankly a mixed experience with much pain and many hurts. But through it all, quite a few people were significantly healed in various areas of their lives; the sense of fellowship within the whole congregation deepened considerably; money and possessions were much more readily shared; and several new and fruitful ministries within the church were created. For about five years, when these households were in existence, we were aware of God's presence among us in unusual ways, and numerous visitors to our church from all over the world spoke about the striking quality of love and joy that they experienced within the whole congregation. Although most of these visitors spoke warmly about the worship, preaching, or whatever, the factor that was mentioned again and again was their experience of the living body of Christ. At that time we might have been most conscious of pain and tears, but through our own profound and acknowledged weakness, the grace of God was even more clearly seen.

A friend of mine, Ken Gullickson, pastor of The Vineyard in Whittier, Los Angeles, once said that our ability to minister is most effective through brokenness, when we are weak, vulnerable, hurting. This creates, he said, a sensitivity to the voice of God and to the needs of others. Nobody naturally wants to be weak, vulnerable, and hurting. We all like to be strong, self-confident, and self-contained. However, it is in the opening of our lives to one another as well as to the Lord that this broken-ness is often effected. It was our experience through household living especially that God broke our natural strength, made us extremely vulnerable, and in this way *his* life and joy were mani-fested, which others were quick to appreciate. When because of our hurts we pulled back from this vulnerability and closed our hearts a little bit to each other (and to God), the sense of God's presence among us was not so obvious. To know "the power of his resurrection" in our midst, we also had to be willing to accept "the fellowship of his sufferings" (Phil. 3:10 KJV).

To begin with each of us contributed financially to the house-hold whatever amount we could. Some paid nothing at all, since they had nothing to offer; others, such as nurses or teachers with reasonable salaries (although still nothing much to shout about admittedly!) gave more than was necessary for their own keep. In this way we were able to support those who had no other means of support. When two other friends joined us, however, they gently challenged Anne and me about the question of finance. It we were really trying to share our lives together, they asked, why not share our money as well—to the extent of no one having a private bank account. We could have a common purse, a household account, into which all earnings went and out of which everyone received exactly the same pocket money. From this, we would have to buy all our clothes, presents (for birth-days and Christmas), and other personal items, such as choco-lates, perfumes, or little luxuries. It seemed a natural extension of our lifestyle, and we shared the idea with our bank manager, who, though puzzled, was slightly impressed (I think) and encouraged us to try it. For several years we worked on this principle, and it became a vital means of release, at least for me, from the constant desire to possess. Covetousness is perhaps the greatest sin of Western culture, and it's also the root of all evil. Community living is not the only way to guard against it, of course, but many of us found adopting this way of life extremely helpful.

We each received $4.50 a week (our children had more lim-ited pocket money). Out of this amount we had to buy every-

thing that was not supplied by the household account as a basic
necessity for life. This meant that I started hunting around
Oxfam shops for clothes, which for a rector in his early forties
was perhaps a bit unusual. I picked up a few marvelous bar-
gains, some of which I am still using. Otherwise it meant saving
up for weeks before buying a pair of shoes. It also meant choos-
ing presents with great care, and those who had time would
make their own Christmas and birthday presents, trusting the
inspiration of the Spirit, and often with much greater satisfac-
tion all around. We also tried to eat less, buy food in bulk, and
shop carefully. We cut out altogether the expense of meals in
restaurants, and learned to celebrate birthdays and festivals at
home. These were often marvelous occasions; it's surprising
how creative a small community can be!

Our household was not only concerned about itself, however.
We attempted in some small measure (we knew that it was only a
pathetic gesture) to identify ourselves with the poor in this
world. We gave money for the relief of the poor and for the work
of the church. Added to that, through this shared life and common purse, we were able to release several members of the
household for full-time work in St. Michael's. For some time
there were only three wage earners in our house, including me,
but five full-time workers in the church, supported entirely by
the household. Without this means of supporting people, some
of the most significant developments in and from the church
might never have come into being. For several years there were
more than thirty full-time workers in the church, many of them
living simply by sharing in these small communities. Some of
these people were involved in the developing special ministries
in the church while others served as lay pastors, secretaries,
youth workers, and so forth. In other words, the households,
beginning with our own, were rapidly becoming the facilitating
ministries that Anne had longed for, and these were benefiting
not only St. Michael's, but also the wider church.

Naturally there were real problems in this type of life. Our
respective parents found it difficult visiting us in such a full
house and sharing us with so many others. Our Christmas gifts
for them, too, were a little meager compared with previous

years, until we started to think through the continued importance of family relationships. Our children initially responded
well to all the new additions to the family, but we made the
mistake (until we realized it) of having too many disturbed people in our home at one time. Indeed, many people believe it to
be a basic principle that you should have no really disturbed
person in your house, if you can help it, when your children are
under twelve years of age, as ours were. Thus the time we spent
with other members of our house began to take its toll on our
children. One day my son's grandfather saw him put a few pen-
nies into a box. "What are you doing with those?" he asked.
Guy replied, "I'm saving up enough money so that we can buy
a house where Mummy, Daddy, Fiona, and I can live *by ourselves!*" It was amusing, but that little remark touched our hearts
and the message got through. However, this lifestyle brought
obvious benefits to our children, too. Members of our household
gave Fiona some musical training and encouraged her in her
schoolwork, particularly math, physics, and chemistry which
became her main interests. Others helped Guy with projects in
our workshop and assisted him with his homework. I suspect,
too, that both our children learned to relate to others better as a
result of their experiences in this larger household.

The most serious tensions of community living came in our
own marriage. It was quite some time before we found anything
close to the right balance between the special relationship within
marriage and the strong brother-sister relationships we were trying to deepen within the household. Not a few crises developed,
and it really seemed that our marriage would fall apart altogether on several occasions. It really was that serious. I was torn
in various directions, and began to suffer from quite deep
depression, which has afflicted me from time to time since then.
None of these problems can be blamed on the "community lifestyle," but only on the sin in our own hearts. It was especially
painful for me (and I suspect for others too) to find that sin was
such a reality and not just a theological issue, and that, for all my
supposed spiritual maturity, I was as weak as any other person,
but for the grace of God.

Miraculously God's grace won through. After numerous

agonizing experiences and with the wise, patient counsel of some good friends, especially David and Jean Smith (elders in our church), Anne and I came through to a richer and deeper relationship than we had ever known since our wedding. Now that we had gone through such storms, when everything seemed to be collapsing around our ears, we discovered a new and stronger commitment. We learned to be much more open to one another, sharing quickly anything that might previously have caused unspoken tensions. Although our eight years in an extended household were sometimes incredibly painful and humbling, we look back now and see that through the tears God was refining and healing us and making us more whole. Also, those years were so fruitful, both in the lives of individuals and in the life of the church, that I am sure we would do it all over again. Anne and I are therefore immensely grateful to all those who shared with us over the years: for loving us, forgiving us, correcting us, being patient with us, and revealing to us more of Christ. In its own peculiar way, this was perhaps the most important period of our lives.

Those who remain cautious if not critical of community households sometimes say, "When you think of households, you think of problems!" But there are often just as many problems within nuclear families (see the enormous tragedy of broken homes today). The difference is that not everyone knows about them in the early stages; it all takes place behind closed doors. In an extended household, however, you feel as though you are living in a shop-window. You have to be real since there is not much that you can hide. "It's not convenient," said a friend of mine, "but it is fruitful!"

Together with moments of pain, we had plenty of fun and great joy in our household. We joined together in Israeli dances on the rectory lawn; we went to the sea together and walked on the Yorkshire moors together. Even the animals felt part of our family—we had a cat, a dog, a rabbit, and two parakeets.

Throughout our years of living this way, I discovered a quality and depth of relationships in Christ beyond anything I had known before. I still have a profound love for all those who lived with us, and I shall always feel a family affinity with them deeper than the ordinary levels of Christian fellowship. The apostle Paul once wrote to those at Thessalonica, "We loved you dearly—so dearly that we gave you not only God's message, but our own lives too" (1 Thess. 2:8 TLB). Such sentiments became a living reality during those years.

Jeff Schiffmeyer, Rector of the Church of the Redeemer, Houston, Texas, once said that "the effectiveness of our ministry depends on the fervency of our love for one another." The experience of shared relationships in Christ proved exceptionally creative in the life of our church, and from this stemmed a number of strategic ministries that God, in his mercy and grace, has used in various parts of the world.

13

Creative Arts
in Worship

I HAD BEEN AT A STUDENT LEADERS' CONFERENCE for four days, and my mind was reeling with all the talking and studying that we had done. Intellectually it had been valuable, but spiritually I was feeling distinctly dry, and it was obvious that I was not the only one. I approached the leader of the conference: "We've been here for four days, and yet we haven't once really worshiped God." He readily agreed, and announced that there would be half an hour of hymn singing before the next session. My heart sank. Yet I had to admit that this had been my own perspective for many years; worship was the part of the service that came before the sermon—a few hymns and psalms and prayers.

Gradually I had come to see the significance of the truth that worship is our primary calling. The chief end of man is "to glorify God and to enjoy him for ever," as the Westminster Catechism expressed it. The difficulty was finding how, in practical ways, we could develop worship so that it became the most important part of our life as a local church. During our first seven years in York we were limited by an organist who was totally reliable and faithful, but not really in tune with the spiritual aims that we were pursuing. When he left, he was replaced for a short time by a brilliant organist who was absolutely committed to Christ, but who was musically too sophisticated for our congregation. He produced amazing harmonies and I found much of his playing exciting. But I could see some puzzled expressions on the faces of those who were trying to sing the straightforward tune. I learned then that a natural talent becomes a spiritual gift only when it both glorifies Christ, *and* edifies the body of Christ. Many gifted musicians (and other artists) have to learn how to serve others with their gifts, rather than use them as a means of self-fulfillment. No doubt it is good for congregations to be stretched occasionally in their musical experience, but Jesus taught his disciples to wash each other's feet, and preachers, instrumentalists, singers, actors, writers, architects, and others all have to learn exactly the same lesson. Unless one's contribution is helping and encouraging others, however brilliant it may be, it will never be a spiritual gift. It will be performance, not ministry. The style of worship that is especially needed today (and is all too rare) is one that is marked by gentleness and simplicity.

The real start of a new dimension in worship for us came when I was away in New Zealand for eight weeks. I was having a tremendous time touring various universities with Merv and Merla Watson, two superb musicians and singers from Canada, whose praise and worship had thrilled me during the International Conference at Guildford two years before. Their music also attracted many New Zealand students, and we saw young men and women turning to Christ having sensed his presence before listening to his Word. At Dunedin we held a lunch time meeting in the students' union, and it was clear from the start that a significant group of students was out to wreck the event. They made a lot of noise and handed out anti-Christian literature that was aggressive and obscene. Through Merv and Merla's continued praise, however, they quieted down considerably, and after I had been speaking for five minutes or so, the leader of the group turned to those who were still talking and said, "Will you shut up? I want to listen to this guy!" There was a respectful silence for the rest of my talk, and I was able to pray a prayer of commitment for those who were ready to receive Christ. There was absolute stillness, and at least two students found Christ that day.

While we were still in New Zealand, my wife back at St. Cuthbert's brought a small group together to sing something during one of our family services, simply to encourage a lay pastor who was preaching his first sermon. The group consisted of Anne, who only sometimes sings in tune, our two children (aged 6 and 4) who played the guitar and triangle, a violinist, and two other guitar players. Significantly they were all members of our household, so that Anne's vision for the households to be facilitating ministries within the church was being fulfilled. Added to that, this very first singing group developed out of the harmony of the members' lives together, not just the harmony of their music. This we later found to be a fundamental principle which can transform any presentation by a singing group or choir from a musical performance (of whatever excellence) into a spiritual ministry which brings the presence of Christ to other people. In order to back this group wholeheartedly, and to be personally identified with it, I even joined it myself for a Sunday or two, playing a borrowed guitar. I could play only three chords, and so gladly stepped down when another guitarist offered his services. The congregation loved this fresh approach to worship, and before long a more competent group was established.

My wife stayed with the original group for some time. Having the vision for this development in worship, she urged the musicians to serve the congregation with their gifts, encouraged and supported the leader of the group, and stressed both the strong commitment and the sharing of lives that such a ministry demanded. All those who were willing to lead the Sunday worship in this way had to commit themselves to an evening of rehearsal each Tuesday, and, as the group became more established, the first hour of that evening was spent in prayer and in sharing together what the Lord had been doing in their lives.

Only as they became more open to one another in God's presence could the Spirit bind them together in God's love; and only as they learned "to live in such harmony with one another, in accord with Christ Jesus," could they together "with one voice glorify the God and Father of our Lord Jesus Christ" (Rom. 15:5-6). Their vision was not just to sing songs, old or new, but to refresh people with the life and joy and love of Christ. Thus, this first hour on Tuesdays of prayer, praise, and sharing was an indispensable part of their ministry on Sundays. Added to that they had to be willing to come about an hour early before each service on Sundays in order to pray and prepare themselves for leading in worship. Any preacher will know the importance of prayerful preparation for his sermon. Yet, if worship is the primary calling for the Christian, our preparation for worship must be equally demanding if it is not to degenerate to "that part before the sermon."

Soon we discovered the necessity of a worship committee, which met each Monday for an hour or two (before the singing group rehearsal on Tuesday), to plan in detail every part of the worship for the coming Sunday. Our aim was to combine the old and the new, and so to produce an appropriate blend of the more familiar hymns with the less familiar spiritual songs that were emerging. Our organist by this time was Andrew Maries, who was also an extremely gifted oboist, and a member of our household. He was the natural leader of the singing group and, with the financial support of the household, became our first full-time musical director. With Andrew, the singing group, and the worship committee sharing responsibilities, we were able to give much more serious attention to the whole area of worship, and it undoubtedly became one of the most essential ingredients in the life of our congregation. After a visit to the church for a week, one Anglican nun wrote: "More than anything I am filled with thanksgiving for what I saw and heard of the worship of St. Michael's, not only in the church building, but in the whole life of the community. I came away with the impression of a Christ-centered, loving, caring, and joyful community." No worship can be taken for granted, and of course we had our ups and downs; but as we set our hearts to glorify God, the sense of his presence in our midst touched the lives of countless people.

Being a musician, Andrew wanted to encourage other musicians in the congregation in their worship of God. This had already been done to some extent before Andrew became our organist, but under his leadership a family service orchestra developed, consisting mainly of children who came regularly to that service. They played recorders, clarinets, oboes, violins, guitars, and even a glockenspiel. Older musicians, apart from those in the singing group, found it harder to make a regular commitment to the evening service, but Andrew drew them together in a special orchestra for the minster guest services and other festive occasions. It was wonderful seeing more and more of the congregation, young and old alike, taking an active part in the service instead of just sitting in their pews.

One further expression of worship that I had not even remotely considered was dance. I knew that the psalmist talked often about praising God's name with dancing, and I remembered that King David had "danced before the Lord with all his might." But I thought this Jewish exuberance of Old Testament days surely was not for respectable Anglicans of today. Added to that, I had loved ballroom dancing before my conversion, but after my conversion I felt that it was one of the many things that the good Christian should not do. So I cut it out of my life altogether. The thought of introducing dance in any form into worship seemed out of the question. Indeed it was never an issue—until Merv and Merla Watson came to York, at my invitation, bringing with them from Canada a remarkable group of seventy professionally trained instrumentalists, singers, *and dancers*. I organized two festivals of praise for them in York Minster, and they were glorious evenings. For the first time I saw dance in worship and found it, to my surprise, quite beautiful and spiritually moving, a descant in movement. Never before had I experienced such a majestic act of celebration. It seemed almost a glimpse into heaven, with the glory of God filling the minster, and I found my spirit lifted up into exalted praise and joy. I soon discovered that many others had been deeply affected by those two festivals. A group of women of varying ages approached me to see if they could use our church hall to learn how to worship God in dance, and cautiously I agreed.

To begin with, however, I had to be sure that dance in worship was biblical. I could see plenty of references in the Old Testament, but where was there any suggestion that dance was a part of the New Testament church? Wasn't this a dangerous idea, bringing the world right into the church? Wouldn't a dance group of attractive women raise all sorts of unholy emotions in the men, no doubt including me? Surely this would detract from true worship, rather than add to it? Might we not be setting an unfortunate example which could lead other churches astray? These were the pressing questions which I had to face before I could possibly encourage a new area of worship that was virtually unheard of at that time. My information may have been limited, but I knew of no other church in the world where dance was used in worship.

As I began to study and pray, a number of pointers helped me to see the way forward. First, dance had clearly been part of the worship of God's people for many centuries before Christ; it would be strange if it suddenly ceased the moment Jesus came to bring fullness of life and joy. Second, the New Testament church used the book of psalms as their hymn book; it seems unlikely that they sang the psalmists' words about praising God with dancing, yet never danced, especially when they had done it throughout their history. Third, there is no New Testament reference to the use of musical instruments in worship, yet very few Christians would question that dimension of worship. Fourth, dance is mentioned twice by Jesus, both instances being significant. In the story of the prodigal son, everyone was happy when the prodigal came home—except the older brother: "As he came and drew near to the [father's] house, he heard music *and dancing*" (Luke 15:25) and he did not like it. On the whole it has been the "older brother" in the Father's house who has taken exception to these "new" forms of worship. Also, Jesus said elsewhere: "To what then shall I compare the men of this generation . . .? They are like children sitting in the market place and calling to one another, "We piped to you, and you did not dance" (Luke 7:31–32). Whatever we do, you respond negatively and critically.

Anne Long has put it this way, "There are those who are very scared of anything moving in a service—either emotionally (such as the sermon) or physically (such as the kiss of peace or a dance). Some want a service that is safe and completely predictable where they can keep their liturgical masks in position and not relate to others. Certainly meeting each other in the presence of God can be very embarrassing if people are unsure about either God or each other." That sums up much of the negative reaction to anything new in the church today. Many Christians are not at all secure in the unchanging love of God, otherwise they would be willing to try any fresh approach that sought to glorify him. Instead they try to find their security in the unchanging structures of the church as an institution. Sooner or later this will always quench the Spirit of God, who is the Spirit of movement.

What about unhelpful sexual emotions being stirred by watching pretty women dance? Obviously this is a danger, and the dancers must aim for modesty in their dress and movement. But I am told, on good authority, that some women have the same sexual problems with certain preachers in the pulpit! What should those preachers do? Hide in the vestry and put their sermons on tape? Surely we must all come to terms with sexuality, since God made man in his own image, both male and female. Some men have been so afraid of sexuality that they relate very badly to women altogether. Indeed I would say that the church in general has become almost gnostic in its attitudes toward the body, treating it as though it were evil in itself. Much of Western Christianity ignores the body altogether, suppresses the emotions, and concentrates almost exclusively upon the mind. But God wants our bodies to be the dwelling-place of his Holy Spirit, and it is by presenting our bodies to God that we offer him spiritual worship.

With these thoughts beginning to formulate, I encouraged the dancers at our church to prepare an interpretive dance to a song of praise. As with the singing group, they met together each week, and for the first hour gave themselves to prayer and sharing from the Scriptures. It was only in the quality of their relationships together in Christ that the dance could be genuinely an act of worship. None of the dancers had any professional training, although one older member had an obvious vision for this ministry and was able to help them with exercises and basic movements. Soon several dances were choreographed to songs of worship. I tried to encourage the group further by teaching the whole church more specifically about worship, referring to the place of dance and giving it plenty of biblical support. I also went to that first hour of prayer and sharing every week (as I did with the singing group) to demonstrate that I was with them all the way, and would back them up should any negative remarks be made.

At first, most of the congregation was as cautious about dance as I had been myself. But gradually, as we pressed on gently with it, explaining all the time what we were doing and why, this expression of worship was not only accepted but well received, and often proved a vital means of communication to the hearts of those present. One Baptist minister wrote to us these words: "I appreciated the worship very much indeed. Except that I felt like crying all the time! You ought to issue tissues at the door! One morning when I was practicing being a 'block of concrete,' the Lord used this dance to cause me to break up and allow his Spirit to come through." That has frequently been the comment from people whom God has touched through dance in worship.

We were convinced that every area of life needs to be redeemed for Christ and that, since God is Creator as well as Redeemer, all the creative gifts of his Spirit, including the performing arts, can be used to his praise and glory. With this conviction we went on with the dance despite some cautious warnings and negative criticisms, usually from those who had never seen it. I soon realized that most of these criticisms were fears, and I received very few negative comments once people had seen for themselves what we meant by this highly explosive word "dance!" It was one of those times when we were sensitive to all comments and fears, but we were not willing to be deflected from developing more effective methods of communication in this highly visual and largely word-resistant age.

After a slow and hesitant start, dance became a natural part of our worship almost every Sunday. We learned a number of vivacious Israeli dances which we performed outside the church when the weather was warm enough. These always attracted quite a crowd of people, including tourists of many nationalities. "What is going on?" they would ask. "Is it a celebration? Is it a festival? Is it a wedding?" It was the golden opportunity to say, "Yes, we are celebrating that God is among us, and that we have come to know him through Jesus Christ." In this way many became genuinely interested and wanted to know more, and some were undoubtedly brought to Christ, initially through the dance. During the summer months, for several years when the Spirit seemed to be with us in unusual power, we had lunch together in the church hall every Sunday, with many visitors joining us. We would then go into a courtyard outside the hall for a time of more Israeli dancing. These proved to be wonderful community dances, both expressing and increasing our sense of oneness together in Christ. Always these spontaneous and joyful moments of celebration drew in the tourists. Although I loved to dance with everyone else (my past love for dance was being redeemed for Christ!), I spent most of the time talking to tourists about the Lord, and had the privilege of leading several to Christ. Once again, they became interested initially through the dance.

As the Spirit seemed to move freely among us, it was a time of remarkable creativity. Another example of this was the making of banners. One girl in our household had obvious artistic gifts and we encouraged her and others like her to use their gifts to the glory of God. A small group of women spent much time in prayer and meditation on the Scriptures, and out of this, one or more of them would have a picture in mind for a banner. This they subsequently created, often linking it up with the theme of a forthcoming service, or one of the great festivals in the church year. Several banners were hung on pillars of the church, and their dignity and beauty greatly enhanced the atmosphere of celebration. The few words on each banner increased the sense of expectancy the moment people came into the church to worship. As more and more banners were made, it was possible to choose, for each service each Sunday, just the right banner for the theme of that service. Sometimes those who came with special needs would find that meditating on the words and picture of a banner was one of the most helpful aspects of the service.

Perhaps the most striking development of artistic gifts came in the area of drama. While leading several university missions I had begun to experiment with other methods of communication in addition to speaking. I came across one or two short dramatic readings and at various universities asked if there were any Christian actors who could do them for me. During a mission at Oxford University in 1973 one student, Paul Burbridge, did one of these readings brilliantly, and it made a considerable impact on all those present as well as enriching my talk that evening. Paul and I began to strike up a personal friendship. At about the same period I was preaching at Cambridge University and had dinner with a close and long-standing friend of Paul's, Murray Watts. We had an immensely stimulating conversation about the arts in general, and I discovered that Murray was a dramatist and had already written one or two plays. Moreover, Murray and Paul had just started a street theater group called Breadrock, and with a group of like-minded friends spent part of their summer vacation performing their sketches, mostly enacted parables, at a seaside resort in North Wales. In this way, they were able to go among the crowds of vacationers and present the gospel in attractive, humorous, and lively ways that were much more readily accepted than an old-fashioned open-air evangelistic service. Although I had never seen the group in action, I was fascinated by the concept, and saw the potential for marvelous communication in this generation that has been so influenced by the drama of television. I could see that Christian artists today could become front-line missionaries in our modern culture, since they have learned the language of communication for the mass of ordinary people right outside the church.

I was also very much aware that Christian artists are under enormous pressure from the secular world in which they spend most of their time, and that the church in general had neither understood them nor done anything much to encourage them. The Arts Center Group in London had been formed a few years before, and was doing excellent work trying to reach artists for Christ, and then seeking to strengthen them in their faith; but the need for supportive churches was obvious. I wondered if in York we could start another Arts Center Group for the north of England. Also, now that we had moved our main services from St. Cuthbert's to St. Michael-le-Belfrey, I wondered if St. Cuthbert's might be used for such a center, maybe even becoming a small theater where people like Paul and Murray could perform their plays. We spent some time thinking, talking, and praying together about the possibilities.

I kept in close touch with Paul during his time in Oxford, and when he got his degree he joined our household for a year. We all became very fond of him, and he was a wonderful, creative member of the community. I especially enjoyed taking him with me on most of my visits to schools and universities during that year. We had some marvelous fellowship together in Christ. Paul was both sensitive and caring, and his infectious sense of fun helped to release some of the tensions in the work or in the household. Even though Paul was much younger than me, I found it extraordinarily helpful sharing closely with a Christian friend in this way. Over the years I have treasured one or two particular friendships like this where I can be completely open and honest about my own needs, questions, and problems.

Wherever we went I would speak, and Paul would illustrate my talks with some very effective, short, punchy, pieces of drama. Occasionally Murray would join us. I led another mission to Oxford University in 1976, and before each talk to a packed-out audience in the Union Debating Chamber, Paul and Murray would perform one of their sketches. The undergraduates simply loved these. A wonderful rapport was established, with spontaneous applause at the end of each sketch. After these pieces of drama I found it so much easier to speak, and it was an exceptionally profitable mission, with roughly 150 students finding Christ. I became increasingly excited about the value of drama in evangelism. It had its own immediate appeal, and cut quickly through the huge barriers of communication that often come between the church and the world. Of course, it is only the Spirit who can bring anyone to Christ, but I could see that the Spirit was using this method of presenting the gospel with considerable effect.

Paul and Murray were beginning to think seriously of developing a theater company, and they felt that York could be the ideal base. The city had a long history of arts festivals, including the medieval mystery plays, and it was not saturated by other theater companies as was the case in London. Added to that, they could see that St. Michael's could give them the spiritual support they would need, and indeed the households that had been established could provide for them financially also. This, in fact, was just what the households did, and it proved the crucial factor in everything else that followed. But for those households supporting the members of the company in every way for the first year or two, the venture would never have been born. Once again we saw the vital facilitating ministry of these households.

I was as excited by Paul and Murray's vision as they were themselves, and I gave them every encouragement I could. In order to achieve some credibility in the eyes of the church before going on with their plans, both of them went for a year to St. John's Theological College in Nottingham for a post-graduate diploma in theology. It was during this time that their vision began to unfold further. As the original street theater group Breadrock they were invited to perform a number of their sketches at the Nottingham Evangelical Anglican Congress (the congress where I was almost lynched by some delegates who had misunderstood my remarks about the Reformation!). Their drama was extraordinarily well received by the large number of Christian leaders who had gathered. Many of these leaders gave them much personal encouragement, and it became clear that their work would receive much wider church support than just from our church in York. "Your sketches are hermeneutically sound!" said a professor of hermeneutics, with even a hint of enthusiasm.

During that year at St. John's, Paul and Murray, together with others from St. Michael's, joined me on missions that we led in Belfast, Leeds, and other places. These missions demonstrated the effectiveness of our "multimedia" approach. We could see that God was beginning to open up for us a sphere of ministry that was much wider than any of us had conceived.

On September 1, 1977, after that year at St. John's, the Riding Lights Theater Company was born. Paul, the director, and Murray, who was mainly an associate member and free-lance writer, were joined by three others from the start: Nigel Forde, Dick Mapletoft, and Sarah Finch. Nigel had lived in York for a number of years, and both he and his wife Hilary had been converted through our church about a year before this. For about ten years Nigel had been a professional actor and writer, and director of the Humberside Theater, Hull. He gave them just the necessary professional experience that they needed at this stage. Dick Mapletoft was a social worker who was a "natural" in many of the comedy sketches, and who had the gift of quickly winning people's affection. Sarah Finch was an extremely talented young actress who had recently finished her training at Manchester. She possessed vitality, a marvelous voice, and unusual sensitivity. Two months later, Geoffrey Stevenson, an American friend working in our church, joined them. (After several years with the company he has since become an accomplished and well-known mime artist.) Then, on January 1, 1978, the company was completed by Diana Lang, who had taught drama at Roedean, a girls school. Diana had much obvious talent and versatility, and was a perfect match for Sarah Finch.

To begin with, all of the company's members were living in households, except for Nigel and Hilary Forde who had two children and a house of their own. They all saw that their close links with our church in York were basic if the company were to have any spiritual ministry as well as artistic effectiveness. Paul came back to live in our own household, much to our delight, and remained with us until his marriage to Bernadette in July 1978.

During the next year or two, Riding Lights came with me everywhere as I began to lead Christian missions, or festivals as we increasingly called them, in many parts of Great Britain. Along with six other talented members of our congregation (gifted in music and dance) we made many trips together. However, as the work of Riding Lights became more widely known, invitations came pouring in to them from all over this country and from abroad, and sadly I had to release them more and more from the team that I had formed for Christian festivals. I could see that a theater company must fulfill its particular call to the theater, and that we were not able to make the best use of their time and energies on these festivals. We have always remained in very close touch, and after going through all sorts of experiences together—some exciting, some hilarious, and some very painful—the depth of our relationships became unusually strong. However, it was necessary for them to develop their own work. The theater group's wide popularity has been seen by the excellent sales of their books on drama (suitable for church drama groups), *Time To Act* and *Lightning Sketches* (both published by Hodder & Stoughton in England). Added to that, literally hundreds of drama groups have sprung up all over the world, some as a direct result of the vision of Riding Lights. In the secular theater increasing recognition has been given to this company. Riding Lights won two awards for fringe theater in the Edinburgh Festival in 1979 and 1980, and they performed a full-length play for Yorkshire television, which was well received.

Further, this means of communication has enabled Riding Lights to bring the gospel to a variety of situations: churches, cathedrals, city halls, schools, universities, shopping centers, market places, theaters, bars, parking lots, seaside resorts, tourist centers—virtually anywhere. They have found that drama is one of the outstanding means of presenting Christ to those who would normally have no contact with the Christian church. At a mission we held in Oxford University in 1982, and after the very positive experience of the previous mission in 1976 when Paul and Murray came to help me, the whole of Riding Lights took an active part. Each lunch time they held a brilliant revue in one of the colleges, which helped to dispel the false but common conception that Christianity means a narrow form of religious piety. Then, each evening during the eight-day mission, they performed three of their sketches to illustrate the theme of my address. It was so popular that after two nights we had to move to a larger building, and an average of at least 1,000 students attended on each occasion, with many turning to Christ as a result.

As Riding Lights became less available to join me, however, I had to form another team who could travel with me. Although they were less experienced and perhaps less gifted than Riding Lights, we discovered that God was able to use us in many unexpected ways.

14

The Mustard
Seed

"WHY NOT OPEN A SHOP AS PART OF THE CONTINUOUS WITNESS of the church in the city throughout the week?" Many ideas are like passing dreams: they fade with the morning and are forgotten. But occasionally there will be a seminal thought which, like the tiny grain of mustard seed growing into a huge shrub, can become surprisingly influential in the kingdom of God.

Anne and I had been aware that most of the creative developments at St. Michael's were directly relevant for the Sunday worship. These were affecting the lives of a great many people, yet there was not much witness in the city during the week, apart from the lunch hour service during the summer and of course the indispensable daily witness of every Christian at home and at work. We had a number of workers involved with young people, and gave strong support to a coffee house called the Catacombs and to the Detached Youth Work, both of which tried to help teen-agers who were in and out of prison and often on drugs. However, God had placed us in the center of a famous city and we were doing little to reach the tourists for Christ. We also saw that there was no center in the city where Christians from different churches could meet together, thus breaking down some of the barriers existing between those churches.

As a direct result of much prayer about this, we believed that God had given us a prophetic vision, if that does not sound too presumptuous, of a shop staffed by a small community of Christians from our congregation. They would live together in the same style as our own extended household, but with the specific task of serving people in the context of a restaurant and gift shop. The confirmation of this vision came from a study of Isaiah 58, which had also been a theme at a recent parish weekend. In that chapter we read about the calling to share our bread with the hungry and satisfy the desires of the afflicted. We also read, "And your ancient ruins shall be rebuilt; you shall raise up the foundations of many generations; you shall be called the repairer of the breach, the restorer of streets to dwell in" (Isa. 58:12). York had recently been restored with much rebuilding of ancient ruins, and this together with its history going back to 71A.D. had made it quite a tourist attraction. But it was difficult to "dwell" in the city shopping center without owning a shop. We also felt that God was calling us to encourage the spiritual restoration of the city to match its material development. It seemed desirable in every way to run a suitable shop where the work would be dedicated to God as an expression of his kingdom. Steadily God pressed this vision on us.

As we were praying about this, we heard unexpectedly about a building, almost opposite St. Michael's, that could be ideal. On enquiry we discovered that the property was owned by the church commissioners of the Church of England, so we could not buy it, but we could rent it at a straight commercial rate. The building was in a poor state of repair, but it was in the heart of the city. We were aiming to have a non-profit-making organization (or one where any profit would be plowed back into the work of the church), attempting in a gentle way to make Christ known in the city. The shop would be run entirely by members of the Church of England. I confess I was disappointed that the rent was so high considering the purpose for which we wished to lease the building. No doubt the commissioners have a responsibility to be businesslike with the vast areas of property that they own, but I tried hard, in vain, to persuade them to reduce the rent. Considerable sums of money were also needed to put the building into working order, which meant, in part, the addition of stringent fire precautions since part of the shop would be used as a restaurant. All in all this venture required a large financial commitment.

Having found the possible building for the project, our next vital task was to discover someone who would run the business and respond to the immediate financial needs. Our thought was that they would live above the shop and lead a small community who would be willing to serve there. The members of that community, or staff, would receive their room and board plus a small amount of pocket money for their personal spending. This was in line with the simplifying of lifestyle that a number in the church were attempting, and it also meant that the overhead costs of the shop could be kept to a necessary minimum. All this, we felt, would be one valid expression of the kingdom of God.

We clearly required a couple who had vision and the willingness to accept a considerable sacrifice of their own. As Anne and I prayerfully pursued this further, we found the ideal couple in Philip and Wendy Wharton, who had either been converted or come into assurance of their conversion a few years before in the days at St. Cuthbert's. Philip worked for the National Coal Board in Doncaster; Wendy had obvious artistic flair, had worked as a buyer in a department store, and was developing evangelistic gifts. Their three children were grown up. Judith, their daughter, was working in our home at that time and was one of the leaders of the dance group in our congregation. Michael and David, their sons, were mostly away from home. The Whartons lived in a lovely house a few miles outside of York. They had a beautiful garden, which Philip especially found a source of great joy, and Wendy had made the house most attractive in every way.

As Anne and I shared our vision with them, they responded in a marvelous way. After thought and prayer, Philip and Wendy, with the total support of their family, were willing to sell their home in order to rent the property and pay for all the expensive alterations that were necessary before they could move in. As it happened, once they had sold their house, they had to squeeze into another already full household for about nine months before the shop was ready. It was an extraordinary testing time for them all, but through much prayer and holding firm to the vision they all survived.

In May 1976 the Mustard Seed, as the shop was called because of its potential influence from small beginnings, was opened. Philip continued with his job at the Coal Board, to provide some stable income (even though they had sacrificed their property and security to make the venture possible). Wendy managed the shop; Geoffrey Stevenson, the American who was later to join Riding Lights, became the chef; and five or six girls committed themselves to serving there, four of them living above the shop in a small community with the Whartons. The group began and ended each day with prayer, asking God to bring into the shop those of his choice, and praying for wisdom to know when to speak openly about Christ to the customers and when to be content simply to serve them with his love. It was extremely hard work, especially as most members of the staff were actively involved in other aspects of the church's ministry, notably the dance group. Some of them also traveled regularly with the teams I was taking with me to lead Christian festivals in many parts of the country. Occasionally tensions would arise, as was inevitable with most of the staff working and living at the same place, sharing their lives openly together, and often facing much pressure. But visitors and customers frequently spoke about the striking atmosphere in that shop: it was so full of love and peace. Indeed, it was because of the fragrance of Christ in that place, mediated through the quality of their relationships together and created through constant prayer, that many people, directly or indirectly, found the Savior. Sometimes, after the hectic day was over, they held evangelistic supper parties for friends and business contacts; and these were some of the best that I have ever experienced.

The vision of the Mustard Seed as a meeting place for Christians from widely different traditions was also being fulfilled. The Whartons and the staff had excellent relationships with Roman Catholic priests and nuns; the Anglican sisters from the minster used to come regularly, and ministers and members of various churches used to meet over coffee or lunch. I enjoyed taking journalists there for lunch when they wanted to interview me for some article. Always they would ask me, "What is there about this place? It is so friendly, and there is such a sense of peace here!" It was natural for me to explain briefly the basis on which the shop was created, and then go on directly to speak about Christ. On more than one occasion I took my guest across the road to St. Michael's after lunch and had the privilege of leading him to Christ.

With Wendy's creative imagination, there were many other positive sides to the work. Members of our church made banners for sale (mostly smaller versions of the ones we had in our church). Others designed notepaper or an attractive mural for the shop itself. Local craftsmen were given orders by the shop for their pottery, artists for their paintings. There was also a good sale of books and albums, some of which came from members of our fellowship. This venture involved many more individuals than just those working at the Mustard Seed.

Anne and I felt that this was one of the most exciting projects we had so far seen during our first eleven years in York. In spite of some tensions in relationships, which occur whenever people work and live in close proximity, the entire work was creative and wholesome, a marvelous expression of the kingdom of God in contemporary and relevant terms. It was used for evangelism, renewal, and reconciliation—the three burdens that have been closest to my heart for many years. It was encouraging also to see the staff maturing spiritually. Many visitors spoke warmly about their experiences at the Mustard Seed, and increasingly Wendy was asked to guide other towns and cities about similar ventures.

It was therefore all the more shattering three years later when

Anne and I heard, while on holiday with our children in Cornwall, that the Mustard Seed was in danger of closing totally. We could hardly believe our ears.

The archbishop of York, Dr. Stuart Blanch, had encouraged me to take something of a sabbatical in 1979, but with our children still at school and with my being frequently away from home on missions and festivals, we felt that the most we could do was to spend all the school holidays away as a family. This included three weeks in a tiny cottage in Cornwall during what turned out to be one of the wettest summers on record! There we received a telegram from Philip and Wendy asking us to phone them at once. We had grown very close to them and they knew well the pressures we had been under; so for them to cable us in such a way meant that the situation, whatever it might be, was serious.

Having no telephone in the cottage, we stopped at the first phone booth and got through to Philip and Wendy. Thus began the first of the lengthy calls twice every day for the rest of our holiday as we heard about the developments. I was tempted to fly or drive back at once (and maybe should have done so—I am still not sure), but my sense of responsibility to Anne and the children, together with the Archbishop's instructions, kept us in Cornwall. Also, my seventy-nine-year-old mother was far from well and had to be admitted to the hospital in Winchester, so we felt it was important to stay in the south of England and to visit her for several days on our way home.

By the time we arrived home, however, the problem in York had reached the point of no return, and the Mustard Seed had all but closed. What had been one of the most fruitful and imaginative enterprises I had ever been associated with, had been virtually destroyed in one swift blow. It was almost impossible to believe.

This is not the place for recriminations, and to this day I still do not fully understand the reasons for what happened. I suspect that a number of complex factors were at work simultaneously: personal frustrations and guilt projected into open criticism; a negative attitude on the part of some towards female leaders, especially those having a strong personality; differing views of spirituality beginning to emerge within the church leadership; a general awareness of some of the problems in the Mustard Seed since, as with every household, those problems were readily observable. It is worth adding, however, that to me those "problems" seemed to be very little different from those of any going concern, especially where relationships are open and committed.

Nevertheless, the next two weeks became a nightmare. It all seemed rather like a court trial. Wendy and Philip came before the elders, about twelve of us. We asked searching questions and made critical comments. Some questioned the whole vision of the Mustard Seed. Others cast doubts on its prayerful origin (though prayer had always been one of its most significant factors). Increasingly a vote of "no confidence" was given. All future hopes were utterly dashed.

Even more serious, Philip and Wendy themselves were all but destroyed through the process. Having been with them from the start, Anne and I could feel at least a part of the incredible agony they went through for many months afterwards, and even three years later I could not pass by the premises without feeling the profound ache of past grief in my spirit. The stock on hand, of course, had to be sold cheaply and the property passed on for other purposes. Philip and Wendy were able to stay in their flat above the shop for another two years until they could buy a small house for themselves. But they lost thousands of pounds through their obedient response to the vision which I firmly believe the Lord gave them. It was nothing less than a miracle of God's grace that they were eventually able to forgive and once again become active members of the church which had hurt them so much.

It never helps to apportion blame. The whole sad saga was a vivid and painful reminder that however "renewed" individuals or churches may feel themselves to be, we are all still sinners, in constant need of the Lord's forgiveness, patience, and love. We still hurt one another, sometimes unbelievably deeply, and we still have to go on forgiving one another, as much as seventy times seven, as Jesus taught. The message of the gospel is that of God's grace through human weakness; but human sin can quench the Spirit and hinder God's work, so that Satan, temporarily at least, appears to triumph. Philip and Wendy had always felt it important to submit to the recognized leadership in the church, whether they felt those leaders to be right or wrong. Through their humble submission, astonishingly painful though it was, God later blessed them both with a wider and richer ministry than before. Even the whole church eventually experienced the resurrection that follows crucifixion when God is in control. But the crucifixion was agonizingly real.

The rise and fall of the Mustard Seed brought many of us to our knees as we repented of all the sin and folly that made the nightmare happen. Thus began a refining, chastening process within the whole congregation, although we did not yet know that the most severe fires were still to come.

15
Sharing
Leadership

IT WAS THROUGH THE RECOGNIZED LEADERS IN THE CHURCH that
the Mustard Seed came to a sudden and tragic end. Yet for all
the rights and wrongs of what happened (and it was difficult not
to feel that we had all been wrong), the shared leadership that I
encouraged in St. Michael's was an indispensable part of its
growth over the years.

Often I think that I lack vision (Anne is the visionary in our
partnership), and usually in the past I have had to be prodded
into action either by Anne's prophetic insights or by murmuring
within the church. It's encouraging to realize that even Moses
was sometimes spurred into taking a lead through the murmurings of the children of Israel. When the problems became too
numerous for him, he wisely consulted his father-in-law (which
suggests how serious the situation had become!) and shared his
leadership in an orderly and impressive way. He had 600 leaders
over thousands, 6,000 leaders over hundreds, 12,000 leaders
over fifties, and 60,000 leaders over tens. The total was 78,600
leaders in all. This must have eased his personal responsibili-

ties considerably, providing he was on good terms with all his leaders.

After my first five years in York, with my university work around the country increasingly taking me away, some members of the congregation were complaining that I was not at home enough to see to all the pastoral problems in a rapidly expanding work. From 1967 onwards we had held an annual residential parish weekend away from York. These had always been significant times for welding our congregation close together and for discerning God's direction for us in the coming year. In 1970, 126 came for the weekend and I put them to work in small groups to review the entire work of the church and to pray for the Spirit's guidance. Partly as a result of this, it became clear to me that I had to ask others to share in the pastoral load of the church.

In Acts 6, when there were complaints about Greek widows who were being neglected, the apostles asked the congregation to choose seven men "of good repute, full of the Spirit, and of wisdom" to help with this pastoral need. We are told by Luke that once they reorganized in this way "the word of God increased." I therefore preached about the need for others to share in the work I was doing in the church, and asked the congregation to suggest in writing those who might be suitable. I noted in Acts 6 that the apostles kept the right of appointment in their own hands, even though the congregation was asked to make the choice. I thought this was a wise procedure, as I did not believe that I should opt out of my God-given responsibility over the congregation as a whole. I was sharing my leadership, not dividing the authority of it into a number of equal parts. Further, before taking any action at all I consulted with the parochial church council, since that is the legally elected governing body in any local Anglican church. The council unanimously agreed with the suggested development.

Naturally I prayed much about the choice of "elders" (as we called them), and it was greatly encouraging for me to see that the choice of the congregation exactly coincided with my own personal feelings. In October that year, six men were commissioned by the bishop of Selby to serve as elders in the church. The appointment was only for a year, since it was obviously experimental. I had heard of one, or perhaps two, Anglican churches that had done something similar, but the whole idea was a relatively new one to our tradition. The six elders happened to include the churchwardens and readers, but there was no automatic or "ex officio" qualification. At the time I was still a curate, and therefore could not have another clergyman to assist me in the growing work. Thus I had to call in laymen to take on some of the burden of pastoral leadership. We met regularly together, once every two weeks in those early days, and I found this group immensely supportive.

Although Anne totally agreed with this new move, the practical implications of it were painful to her. Up to this point, in spite of many strains, Anne and I together had been the effective leaders of the work, as we tried to discern God's guidance for each new stage of development. Now that the elders had come into being (and for many years men only were commissioned), Anne was excluded from this leadership group. She therefore had to work indirectly through me, trying to impart through my thick skin some of the creative ideas that she was constantly having. Then I had to work each idea out for myself before sharing it with the elders. In the first century church in Antioch, the leadership of the congregation consisted of a group of prophets and teachers. On reflection, it was ridiculous that we should have excluded for many years the one person who had such a growing prophetic ministry. Indeed it would have been most healthy if that prophetic ministry could first have been exercised within that eldership. But our prejudice against female leaders was strong, and the thought of Anne, or any other woman, joining that group never remotely entered our heads. An official report on our church by the Archbishops' Council on Evangelism (a most thorough report that was extremely searching and helpful) commented about our fellowship: "It is male-administered, female-attended, mother-and-family and student oriented. . . It is directed by men, women being excluded from the eldership but playing a leading role through prophecy. There is a real

danger of compromising prophetic vision where it does not tally
with the going concerns of the eldership. A determined individ-
ualist would find the whole setup frustrating.'' I did not realize
at the time just how frustrating Anne and several others would
find the male domination that had emerged from this otherwise
necessary move.

In spite of all that, the experiment of eldership was clearly
successful, and the elders were subsequently appointed for three
years at a time, subject to reappointment. This allowed a certain
turnover within the eldership, determined partly by age, health,
and other commitments. We were always on the lookout for
those whose primary ministry was pastoral. The church council
was the governing body within the church, and therefore its
main function was administrative; but it happened that most of
the elders were also on the council so that there was never any
friction between the two groups. The council met only five or six
times a year, but the elders were soon meeting every Saturday at
7:00 A.M. and about every six weeks all of Saturday morning
together (later we met at 6:30 A.M. each Tuesday). In Anglican
terms, the eldership was virtually the pastoral subcommittee of
the church council, but that was a clumsy title and we never used
it. Always the elders were commissioned by the bishop of Selby
or the archbishop of York, as we tried to bring the whole scheme
under the authority of the wider church. In effect, the commis-
sioning of the elders was a local ordination for ministry within
our church.

In July 1972 we went one stage further, and one of the elders,
Peter Hodgson, was commissioned as a full-time lay pastor.
Peter had been licensed as a reader for twenty years, and while
running his own radio and television repair business had
enjoyed increasing numbers of conversations about Christ in the
homes where he went on business. He was an invaluable helper
since he had lived in the area all his life, and knew intimately
some of the needs of those who came to us. Our tasks as a church
council were simply to recognize the obvious pastoral gifts that
God had given him, to hear his own sense of calling to full-time
service within the church, and then to commission him for that

purpose, accepting the financial responsibilities of him as a married man with three growing children.

One almost impossible task facing the elders was to put a brake on my own outside engagements. I was slowly learning to say No to invitations, but too quickly responded to opportunities both for evangelism and for the renewal of the church. Some invitations I refused with minimal thought; the others I brought to the elders meeting, and we spent perhaps a disproportionate amount of time sifting through them to see how I should reply. However, for me it was immensely helpful submitting to the combined wisdom of the elders, and since one of them was my doctor, Walter Stockdale, who had looked after my asthmatic problems with great care and skill for many years, the group had good reasons for trying to prevent me from doing too much. Further, since my outside engagements often increased the tensions at home, the elders had a primary pastoral duty to perform towards our family, which was not always easy for them.

Even with the establishment of elders, which greatly eased the pastoral load off my own shoulders, we heard further murmurings within the church after a year or two. The congregation was growing too big, especially since our move into St. Michael-le-Belfrey in 1973. It was hard for people to know one another in any depth; and most people needed to belong to a relatively small and identifiable group. Our Thursday fellowship, which had moved out of the rectory into St. Cuthbert's, had leveled off at about 150, still far too big for any intimate fellowship. Consequently, a few small groups had formed spontaneously so that people could enjoy more relaxed fellowship within the informal atmosphere of someone's home. The time had come to organize these groups in a more structured way, and a half-day parish conference one Saturday confirmed the widespread desire for this to happen as soon as possible. We dealt with this challenge in several ways.

One area that needed immediate strengthening was the young people's group. So in April 1973 I went to see the archbishop of York, Dr. Donald Coggan, to ask if I could have a curate. "But you are only a curate yourself!" he replied. "Are you asking to be made a vicar?" I noticed a slight twinkle in his eye, so I dutifully and accurately answered, "Well, I have been a curate for fourteen years, and I just thought that perhaps. . ." The archbishop was very gracious. On September 19, the day of our wedding anniversary, I was instituted as vicar of St. Michael-le-Belfrey, and four days later my first curate, Andrew Cornes, joined me. I had been used by God to help Andrew find Christ at Oxford University. Later, during his placement with us as part of his training for ordination, I had come to respect Andrew immensely. He had an astute mind, obvious drive, gifts of leadership, and all the marks of a potentially outstanding preacher and teacher. Added to that, his Christian experience at camps such as the ones I participated in at Cambridge gave him excellent training for developing the youth work almost from scratch. One particular problem, however, had to be worked through with honesty. Andrew could not identify with the charismatic renewal (as it was now commonly called). At the same time, my burden was already growing for reconciling Christians over this issue. Since Andrew was crystal clear about the heart of the biblical gospel which I constantly sought to proclaim, I felt that I wanted to invite him to join me. In addition I could see great merit in deliberately inviting as curate someone who was definitely not a "card-carrying charismatic," partly to demonstrate that our unity is always in Christ, and not in any particular spiritual experience apart from that.

As it happened, Andrew had three marvelous years with us. He was loved immediately by everyone, and his gifts were widely appreciated. His sermons were models of careful and spiritual exposition, his sense of humor was infectious, his concern for individuals was full of the compassion of Christ, and, above all, his pioneer work among young people was brilliantly effective. Not only did many young people find Christ through Andrew's ministry, but his follow-up system, based largely on what he had learned at those boys' camps, enabled them to grow rapidly in the faith. Each young Christian was matched with a family (helping to bridge some of the generation gap), and the father and mother of that family would spend an hour a week reading the Bible with the young Christian, as well as extending hospitality through meals. By the end of those three years the young people's fellowship, called Eureka (meaning "I've found it/him"), had grown from noone to about 140, most of whom were steadily maturing in their faith.

In 1976 Andrew left to become director of training at All Souls, Langham Place. I am not sure that he changed his views about charismatic renewal during his time with us, but he was totally loyal, and our relationship together was always one of the utmost harmony and mutual respect. Andrew was replaced by Patrick Whitworth, who had also found Christ during a time I spent in Oxford University. Patrick took on the excellent work that Andrew had established and became more widely involved in the whole church as well. Andrew had spent about ninety-five percent of his time with young people since I saw that as a priority, but I was concerned that Patrick receive more general training. It soon became obvious that God had gifted him both in evangelism and teaching, and it was a joy to share these aspects of the ministry with him. Patrick was also much loved by the whole congregation.

The young people's group was not the only one developed at this stage. We saw that most people wanted, and needed, to belong to a small group (the ideal size being about twelve) where they could get to know one another informally. So we divided the regular congregation into more than twenty *area groups*, called this because the determining factor for including members in them was usually a geographic one. We wanted these groups to build up a sense of community in a given small area, allowing them the opportunity of building and deepening relationships "seven days a week." For example, although the focal point was a meeting in someone's home every other week for the purpose of praise, prayer, study, sharing, and ministry, it was a natural practice in our group for members to walk in and out of each other's homes without needing to knock or ring the door bell. If a visiting group member saw a young mother struggling with laundry, cooking, and babies, they might offer immediate practical help, followed by a helpful chat over a cup of tea and then specific prayer. Mothers who had just given birth found that all their meals were provided for them and often that their other children were looked after, sometimes even overnight in the homes of nearby families. There was also the sharing of property such as cars, washing machines, or lawnmowers. Two women in one group at times did a weekly shopping trip for the whole group. Baby-sitting was offered and meals were cooked for any who were sick. We encouraged the sharing of the whole of our lives, not just Bible study and prayer. Added to that, some people could not come to every meeting (or even at all), but they were still important members of the "community of God's people" in that area, and we wanted them to feel that they belonged.

Each area group had a leader and ideally an assistant leader, since it was our hope that if these groups grew healthily they should be willing to split, multiply, or "bud" every year or two. Some groups, like individuals, were more gifted in evangelism and thus tended to grow more quickly. Others were more committed to ministry within the church. Sometimes the groups were encouraged along specific lines of Bible study, and a number of them had particular prayer projects such as the support of certain missionaries. But all groups were designed for the sharing of lives. Normally this sharing would be personal thoughts drawn from the Scriptures, but occasionally such thoughts would emerge from ordinary events of life. We knew that God is always trying to speak to us, through his Word but also through every circumstance of life, and we encouraged each other to listen to God, hear what he was saying, and then share it with one another. In doing this, it was important for us to be open and real so that within the small group of committed Christians people would feel free to mention quite personal needs, thus drawing out the love, prayer, and support of others in the group. It was in "speaking the truth in love" that we were trying to grow up into Christ in every way.

Another vital aim of these groups was sharing pastoral responsibility. When needs of any kind arose—and they were always doing so of course—the members of the group (not necessarily the leaders) tried to help one another in spiritual or practical terms. Further, each elder had the oversight of two or more of the groups, so that if the pastoral need lay beyond the combined experiences of the group, it was passed on to the elder. Then, if the elder felt inadequate to deal with the problem, he could, with permission, share it with another elder of greater experience. In this way the pastoral load of the church was being borne by a growing number of men and women, thus easing the enormous strain I felt, as any clergyman would with his congregation rapidly increasing in size.

All the elders were members of an area group with people in their geographical area and had responsibility for one or more others; but they were never leaders of those groups, except in emergencies, so as to encourage more and more lay leadership within the church. On one snowy occasion when I was present at my own area group, a young wife apologized that her husband was late getting home from work because of the snow, and she explained that he was to have been the leader for that night. "Oh well," she continued, "I suppose I had better lead it instead of Colin." I was delighted that she did not think of handing the group over to me as rector of the church. Moreover she led it extraordinarily well, and I was greatly refreshed by the whole evening.

Group leadership is a demanding role, and very few of our leaders were naturally gifted in this. We later developed a number of support groups consisting of two or three elders together with the various group leaders for which they were responsible. These individuals met every two or three weeks, and were expected to share their lives together as well, since the way in which they did this in the support group likely would determine the quality of the area groups they were leading. Also, of course, they were able to raise difficulties they were experiencing within their groups, or share certain aspects that they had found valuable; and then they prayed for one another. As with every structure like this, some groups went better than others, and the system wasn't perfect. But the sense of fellowship within the whole congregation grew almost visibly as a result, and the individual needs of the majority had much more chance of being met than if the whole work depended on the feverish activities of one or two hard-pressed clergymen.

It is significant that virtually every major movement for spiritual renewal in the history of the church has been marked by the development of the small group. The amazing missionary impact of the Moravians lay in their constant attention to relationships between one another, based in small groups. John Wesley, who owed his conversion and evangelistic zeal largely to the Moravians, organized his "class-meetings" or "nurture cells," and these became a vital part of the extraordinary influence he had on all of England in his day. The remarkable growth of the Pentecostal Church in South America is also due, in part, to its emphasis on the cell group structure. Numerous other illustrations could be given. Naturally there are dangers. Unless the leaders develop close relationships with one another, these groups can become independent or divisive. Unless the groups see that part of their function is evangelism and service, they can degenerate into unhealthy introspection. Unless the members of the groups develop friendships outside the church altogether, the groups can tragically become safe and comfortable religious ghettos, useless as a witness to the wider world. Unless there is constant training and encouraging of leaders, some groups will quickly die a natural death. Yet, given these and other areas of concern, the sharing of leadership became an indispensable part of the growth and witness of St. Michael's church.

Even this degree of shared leadership, however, was not enough for the growing work. Throughout the seventies my ministry had been steadily widening to various parts of Great Britain and to other countries, and I found it increasingly hard to cope adequately with the demands in York as well. The wider ministry seemed to have the backing of church leaders of most denominations, and we could see that God was using our Christian missions and festivals in many towns and cities, but I could not sustain the pressure indefinitely. My health was not good; my asthmatic attacks required frequent courses of steroids. In addition, the traveling work always imposed strain on our family. Clearly it was not easy for Anne, nor was it much easier for me.

We had invited the Archbishops' Council on Evangelism to study our parish in depth and to make a detailed report on their observations. In November 1977 a team of nine spent a week with us all. They studied our worship and prayer life, our evangelism and pastoral care. They looked into our finances and practical administration. They examined our preaching and teaching, and our work among children, young people, and university students. They spent time in our households and asked searching questions about the area groups, the creative arts groups, and the various methods of communication we used. Every aspect of the work was carefully researched, and most of the comments were exceedingly encouraging. Concerning the creative arts, for example, they stressed that "man does not learn by words alone." They commented that "there are so few congregations as free to experiment in these forms, yet dance, movement, and drama are the very warp and woof of the TV age, the media whereby most adult public communication now takes place." Most important of all, since the subject of concern is the communication of Christ to the world today, the team pleaded for "the continued examination of the most effective blendings of dance, music, movement, drama, participation in liturgical prayer, preaching, and everyday witness *as expressions of the Word within the Body of Christ.*" Helpfully, the team also revealed a number of weaknesses in our church life which needed immediate attention. It was hard not to be threatened by the exercise, yet we all knew that it was extremely healthy for us to be "examined" in this way, especially since so many visitors had been coming to learn from us.

During the week I talked with Canon John Poulton, the leader of the team, and he made a suggestion specifically for me: "Why not bring in someone as vicar to run St. Michael's under your overall leadership, while you become rector, with a greater freedom for traveling?" I had already considered this seriously as a possible solution, so this extra confidence was just what I needed. A slightly similar arrangement had worked for John Stott at All Souls, when Michael Baughen went there, so at least the idea had a precedent.

The question was, who should become vicar? If a newcomer came in, it might be years before he gained the confidence of the congregation, and I knew of no one who was an obvious choice from outside York. However, we had a young clergyman in our congregation, Graham Cray, a traveling secretary with the Church Pastoral Aid Society. Anne and I increasingly began to feel that he might be exactly the right person. He was already an elder of our church and he and his supportive wife Jackie were thoroughly accepted and liked by all in the congregation who knew them. As part of the week with the Archbishop's Council on Evangelism, we had a retreat weekend with our elders and church council members. During that time Anne and I talked to Graham and Jackie at length about the ideas that were beginning to form in our minds. They were a bit overwhelmed, but warmed positively to the idea, and it became obvious to us that they shared our vision for the church and would be able as well to introduce some fresh and helpful elements. I discussed all this with the elders the next day, and it then seemed right to approach the archbishop, Dr. Stuart Blanch, for his advice.

It so happened that the archbishop was due to preach at St. Michael's two weeks later, and I had an opportunity on that evening to raise the issue with him. Immediately he saw the value of the scheme. So plans were put into action, and on July 1, 1978, Graham began as vicar of St. Michael's. Thus began a wonderful relationship between Graham, Jackie, Anne, and myself, as we shared together the primary role of leadership in the church. It seemed as if an immense weight had been taken off my shoulders, and Anne and I valued the gentle loving wisdom of Graham and Jackie more than we could say. We were increasingly impressed by their maturity of vision, their grasp of the gospel in today's world, and their shrewd understanding of the kingdom of God. I have found Graham's teaching brilliant, and I have personally learned much from him over the years.

Sooner than I expected I found myself phasing out of the main role as leader, and with complete confidence letting Graham take over from me. However, change of leadership can be disturbing to a congregation, especially after a lengthy ministry in a church. Our church was no exception to this general rule. What followed proved to be the most painful experience in my entire ministry.

16
Tension & Division

THREE COMMON STAGES OF ANY COMMUNITY are *honeymoon, nightmare*, and then *reality*. Much the same is true also of a new ministry in a church, as our congregation experienced. To begin with, they were overjoyed with our new arrangement. The fresh depths of Graham Cray's teaching touched many people's lives; his constant presence in York was a refreshing change from my increasing absence; and a variety of loose ends in the church were beginning to be tied up. It was largely through Graham's initiative that the area groups were reorganized into manageable sizes, and support groups for the leaders came into being. Time and again I was impressed by his mature grasp of the pastoral needs in the church, and he was clearly a gifted counselor—a fact that many came to appreciate for themselves in the following months.

Nevertheless, the changeover of leadership was, as is often the case, a time when various negatives came into the light, particularly frustrations and criticisms which might have been suppressed out of deference to the previous leader. After a year or so, I became aware that new influences from one or two leaders (not Graham) were beginning to creep in, and they were pulling the church in a different direction. Graham was aware of this as well, but I was not always around to support him. There were some heavy prophecies about God's judgment on our church, and these instilled an unhealthy fear and critical spirit into parts of the congregation. Personally, I questioned whether those prophecies were from the Lord; but, significantly perhaps, they were all given when I was away, and I heard only a recording or report of them when it was too late to do much about them. The boat was beginning to rock. The storm, though, was still only on the horizon.

A little while later, I heard that a number of people within the church had quietly visited a non-denominational fellowship in Ulster, Northern Ireland, and were going back there on other visits, taking their friends with them. There was nothing wrong with this in itself. Indeed, many from throughout Northern Ireland had visited our church on several occasions and apparently were blessed by those visits. But then I discovered that some people in our church were putting themselves under the authority of the leaders of that Ulster fellowship, and those leaders, in turn, were coming under the authority of other leaders in Florida in the U.S. These individuals were apparently looking for a much stronger authority structure, involving a heavy form of disciplining, shepherding, and submission. Moreover, this group in our church was pushing a slightly different aspect of spirituality which had all the dangers of becoming a super-spirituality. The group also questioned the developments of the creative arts within the church, which God had been using with much obvious blessing.

It was possibly due to these emphases that an investigation was also held into Anne's ministry. One or two elders felt that she had been too strong and dogmatic, which, if true at all, was doubtless due to her having spiritual maturity and vision beyond that of most of the elders—particularly frustrating since she was a woman with no voice in the eldership. Up to that point Anne had been a much valued leader of the area group and area fellowship (a larger body comprising about six area groups), a prominent member of the worship committee, and the founder-leader of the Children's Workshop, an exciting and creative group treating children as members of the body of Christ and encouraging them to take a full part in the life of the church at their own level. Anne had also initiated a number of women's groups which had proven to be enormous supports for many women, some of whom were under much pressure domestically.

The result of the investigation was that Anne was required by those elders to withdraw from *all* the groups in which she had been involved for a period of six months at least—although it was difficult to imagine how she could go back into them after six months. Part of the reason given by these elders was that they felt this was needed to strengthen our own marriage relationship, which actually had been steadily improving by that stage. In reality, since I was shortly to go off to Australia and New Zealand for ten weeks (almost half of those six months), the decision was pastorally disastrous. Despite a vigorous protest from both Graham and me, the recommendation somehow went through. For Anne, the spiritual and emotional effect was like an amputation of both her arms and legs. I was amazed to see though, after an initial struggle, how well she accepted it, having always determined to submit to the elders whether she felt they were right or wrong. I was far more angry than she. From New Zealand, I wrote a furious letter to one elder, and later apologized for my outburst.

My tour in Australia and New Zealand was an exhausting one, though filled with numerous encouragements. I shall always remember the best street theater our team ever experienced, in the Cathedral Square of Christchurch. A crowd estimated at 1,000 was gathered and the sense of communication was excellent. An aerial photograph of the event is certainly impressive. Likewise I shall remember our final night in Auckland where, despite my fears and misgivings, the racecourse grandstand was booked. I felt it was the wrong time of year: cold, dark, windy, and threatening to rain. However, the confident faith of the organizers was justified: a crowd of 6,000 to 9,000 turned up (the estimates varied) and streams of people came forward in the dark to say that they had committed their lives to Christ. Altogether on that tour I preached 150 times in fifteen different centers, and the team I went with worked equally hard—Phil and Joy Potter, Liz Attwood, and Pauline Hornby, with local additions helping us out. Our final stop was in Canberra where we had packed-out meetings in the big tent directly in front of Parliament House. Imaginative publicity added to the festival, and I found myself described as a "gentle-mannered rector" and the team as "energetic musicians, dancers, and actors who have leapt across the British scene with a burst of spring fever which lasts all year round." I think the spring fever was sagging a bit by that time, but everywhere we went we were startled to see how God was using our varied presentation of the gospel. Even in the two most discouraging meetings (from our point of view) we heard later how people's lives had been changed by the Spirit of God.

In my telephone calls to York each week, however, I found Anne to be increasingly depressed—not by her removal from all the groups to which she had given her life, but by the tensions and splits developing in the church, particularly within the leadership. There had been more heavy "prophecies," and one or two leaders were clearly trying to swing things their own way. They were accepting neither Graham's leadership, nor, by implication, my own. Indeed, it was an experience during my tour that helped me understand one crucial principle in shared leadership.

In one city I met a minister who told me, after one of my seminars: "David, for years I have been trying to share my leadership. But now I find that they are all pulling in different directions." This very fine man had been the pastor of his church for fifteen years, and God's work there had been an inspiration to Christians all over the country. Now, amazingly, he was experiencing just the same problems that we were going through in York. At the next seminar we discussed at greater depth the whole issue of shared leadership, and saw that the main leader (vicar, minister, pastor) has a God-given "apostolic" role to play, in the same way that Timothy was the apostle of the church at Ephesus. Shared leadership begins with the sharing of lives and building up of deep relationships of love, commitment, and trust. Unless that quality of relationship exists, shared leadership will be fraught with dangers because of the spirit of competition and self-seeking. But even when the fusion of lives has genuinely taken place, there must still be the leader of leaders, and others must respect that God-given call. The other leaders may, in love, question, challenge, or even rebuke this leader if necessary; but in the long run they must submit to the one who is over them in the Lord. The tragedy of the church today, not least in "renewal" circles, is that "every man does what is right in his own eyes." This was the mark of spiritual degeneracy in the Old Testament, and the sign of carnality in the New.

On my return from Australia, I found our church more like the Corinthian church than at any other time during the previous years. At Corinth, various factions had formed around the different personalities of Paul, Apollos, and Peter. This was tragic, wrote Paul, since those leaders were only servants through whom God worked to bring life to others. They were nothing in themselves. Moreover, he said, the one and only foundation for any church is Jesus Christ; it can never be the personality, gifts, or even teaching of a particular leader. Paul went on to say (1 Cor. 3) that it is therefore extremely important how we build on that one foundation of Christ. The whole theme of that chapter is the unity of the church. If we build up anything which becomes divisive, we are building with "wood, hay, straw"—materials which will not last the fiery test of God's judgment. Indeed, if anyone destroys the temple of God, God will destroy him. Paul could not have been more emphatic about the sinfulness of divisions within the church.

I had one brief day off after my ten-week tour, to recover from jet lag and total exhaustion before plunging into a number of intense meetings and discussions. We tried our utmost to avoid a split, however, the splinter group, as it was rapidly becoming, was teaching a dangerous idea currently taught in some circles but with no theological basis. They were distinguishing between the *logos* and *rhēma* of God (both words being used interchangeably in the New Testament for the Word of God). They held that the *logos* referred only to the general Word of God in the Scriptures, but the *rhēma* was the prophetic word, God's word for now. Further, although there may be general agreement about the *logos* of God, our unity and fellowship depends in practice, they claimed, on our response to the *rhēma* of God. One of the leaders of this splinter group wrote to me: "Unity is not built on a relationship with my brother, but on a response to the Word of God. Thus you may have as much unity as you have agreement on the *rhēma* of Jesus Christ." To them, if there was a disagreement in our response to the *rhēma* of the Spirit, it was virtually impossible to maintain any working fellowship. Thus, they concluded, they had no choice but to separate themselves from us.

The subtlety is that all this may sound plausible to the Christian who genuinely wants to be obedient to God. I did not doubt the sincerity of this group. I had known them, loved them, prayed for them, and worked with them for many years. The trouble was that the basis on which they felt they had to withdraw was entirely fallacious. Our unity is, quite simply, in Christ. The New Testament permits us to separate from others *only* if they deny either the divinity of Christ, his death for our sins, or his resurrection from the dead. All this we tried to explain as clearly as we could, both publicly and privately. Graham, again entirely with my support, even asked the main leader of this group to be an elder again when the time came for reappointing elders. This was a final attempt to avoid a split, but the invitation was not accepted.

Perhaps the last crunch came when Graham gave a masterly series of four sermons on leadership and, as vicar but with my total agreement, included three women in the next body of elders, one of those women being Anne. Many of us felt that the inclusion of women was long overdue, but that particular splinter group found this altogether unacceptable. About twenty left the church. Although we were thankful that a much larger group did not split off (we had been told that 150 would leave), the pain was still enormous, especially as we had enjoyed such close fellowship with these twenty for many years

Looking back, I can see that the considerable overlap between my leadership and Graham's was extraordinarily important, and except for that factor the split might have been much worse. I wonder if this should not be the pattern for the transfer of leadership in any church, especially if the previous leader has been there for a long time.

In spite of the prophecies of God's judgment upon us, the shakened and chastened congregation found a new unity in Christ, gave Graham full support once again in his role as vicar, and became hungry for further spiritual renewal. Through the visit of a gifted pastor and great friend of mine, John Wimber (from Yorba Linda, California), we had another Pentecost. At their own expense, John and a team of twenty-nine from his congregation came, and the Spirit of God worked through them with unusual effectiveness and power. There were some wonderful healings and conversions, and many were filled with the Spirit. Those who had recently separated themselves from us kept away; but among the rest of the congregation there was a marvelous healing of relationships where tensions still existed. John Wimber, whose own church had grown from almost nothing to 4,000 in four years, and who has wide experience of churches in many places, told me that he had never found any other church like ours that was hurting so much. The sense of grief was acute. Because of the special depth of shared relationships that God had given us in Christ, the split had caused terrible wounds. Through this we felt, no doubt in very small measure, the pain that Christ must feel over the divisions in his body, the church, today.

Those who leave their churches to form "non-denominational" fellowships need to realize what they are doing. As soon as those fellowships become more structured and administer the sacraments of baptism and the Lord's Supper, they virtually become a church, and when those "house churches" begin to have some affiliation with one another, another denomination is born. This is the sad but constant witness of church history, but we never seem to learn the lessons of

the past. Again, I believe, as in Ezekiel's vision, that God's purpose is not to replace but to renew the dry bones of existing
Christian traditions, and I see God doing this with denominations throughout the world today. Often I say to those who are
impatient with the stuffiness of their traditional church: "If you
want more life, give your life; if you want more prayer, give your
prayer; if you want more love, give your love..." It is only as the
grain of wheat falls into the ground and *dies* that it will bring
forth a harvest.

There is often an unholy impatience when Christians split off,
often on some minor issue, to do their own thing. It is worth
reflecting that Jesus continued worshiping in the synagogue and
temple for some thirty years, patiently bearing with its spiritual
deadness, before his incredible and brief ministry took place.
The only divisions that are in any way justifiable are those that
occur when Christians are literally driven out of their churches
through active persecution, as Wesley and Whitefield were
(though they did their utmost to remain within the Anglican
church throughout their lives), or when the institutional church
has apostatized by denying the most fundamental tenets of the
Christian faith. All other divisions are wrong and sinful, and
they grieve the Holy Spirit of God. We need only to read the
urgent apostolic appeals for unity within the New Testament
epistles to understand how important this is.

If we really followed the Spirit we would be willing to go
through suffering and crucifixion if need be—no doubt at the
hands of religious people—in order to bring life to others. To
form another church of like-minded people, thereby impover-
ishing the lives of our brothers and sisters who are working hard
for renewal within their own churches (however slowly and
imperfectly), is an easy option and not the way of Christ.
Indeed, it is a sad twist that those who genuinely want to "obey
the Spirit" can so easily "grieve the Spirit" by their actions,
which are contrary to the Word of God.

Naturally at St. Michael's there were faults on our side too.
No doubt we should have been more renewed, more prayerful,
more committed, or whatever. In one sense this will always be

true. In any painful split like this, no one can point the finger; everyone needs the mercy and forgiveness of God. We are all in the wrong. The amazing truth is that, in spite of our sinful divisions God can overrule what we do to one another (and to him) so that his kingdom grows even more. The apostle Paul once had an argument with his great friend Barnabas. Luke tells us in Acts 15 that "there arose a sharp contention, so that they separated from each other; Barnabas took Mark with him and sailed away to Cyprus, but Paul chose Silas and departed" (vv. 39–40). It seems that the church expanded still further as the result of God's mercy and grace in the midst of human sin.

17
Renewal Weeks for Leaders

"Go on talking," I said. "I think the Lord is saying something through you." I began to scribble notes as fast as I could. I was at the sharing time of the dance group, and one member of that group was talking quietly about her thoughts concerning possible future developments in York. As Sue talked, I sensed that what she was sharing was prophetic in its quality. This was in the summer of 1976.

During the previous three years, since our move into St. Michael-le-Belfrey, many church leaders from Great Britain and overseas had visited our church to see what we were learning about evangelism, renewal, and church growth. Occasionally those visits, brief and seemingly insignificant, had resulted in the transformation of people's ministries, much to our surprise. However, although we felt it right to give time to clergy and other leaders, we were hearing the same questions over and over again, and we found it a time-consuming business repeating the same answers. I seemed to be even less available for my own congregation, and though the time spent with one visitor after another was nearly always profitable, the demands being made on me and on some of the other elders were proving a problem.

"Why don't we plan a special week, perhaps twice a year," asked Sue, "when we invite lots of leaders to our church, let them stay in the homes of the congregation, experience the life of the fellowship, and see for themselves the strengths and weaknesses? Then several of us could share in seminars what we are trying to learn." The whole vision excited me. Not only would this concentrate our time with visitors into two main weeks in the year (with some exceptions for overseas visitors), but it would allow those who came to see much more in depth God's work among us than I could ever begin to explain in the course of a few hours. Instead of the congregation finding that much of my time was being absorbed with those outside York, they themselves would be directly involved in sharing any vision that God had given us.

The elders were enthusiastic about the idea, and two prophetic words were later given, confirming that God wanted to use us as a source of encouragement and renewal for other churches. But for this initiative from the Lord (as I took it to be), I would never have dared to launch these weeks for local church renewal. Who were we to tell other churches what to do, even by implication? Those of us in the hot seat of leadership were profoundly aware of numerous weaknesses in our own congregation. We ourselves were in constant need of spiritual renewal and greater maturity. In fact, I was later delighted when I received a letter from a Swiss pastor: "We had heard that St. Michael-le-Belfrey was an almost perfect church. We could hardly believe it, but we praised the Lord. Now we have been to York personally, now we have seen. It is not perfect, and now we praise the Lord even more. If the Lord can use sinners such as the people in St. Michael-le-Belfrey, he can use us too!" That was clearly the good news we had to share: if God could do something among us, he could do something anywhere!

In many ways, this proved to be the strength of our Renewal Weeks, as we called them. The first took place in April 1977. Although we did not advertize it at all, word got around and we were inundated by requests for reservations. We went on to organize two of these weeks each year (in April and September for six days at a time). We held twelve in all, with some 1,500 coming from all over the United Kingdom and from many countries overseas. We had especially large numbers from Northern Ireland, Wales, and Sweden. Most of the participants were leaders, since we always stressed that these weeks were designed for them particularly, and those who came represented many traditions and denominations. The main difficulty we had was finding sufficient hospitality to accommodate all those who wanted to come. We observed an undoubted momentum of the Spirit, which confirmed our discernment about God's initiative in the whole venture.

These weeks took a simple form, and were superbly managed by Douglas Greenfield, a businessman who was one of our elders, and by his wife Joan. Normally guests arrived on Friday evening and settled into the homes where they were staying. Some of the hosts had never received guests before, and one or two embarrassing situations had to be sorted out quickly—we had the occasional complaint of impossible beds or bedroom doors that would not shut. Other hosts were so generous in their hospitality that their guests found this experience of loving relationships the most refreshing part of the week. On Saturday morning we took time to explain some of the biblical principles behind renewal, particularly giving an indication about what the guests might expect in the Sunday services, since our developments in terms of music, dance, and drama were quite new, even revolutionary, for some of them. On Saturday evening we usually had entertainment, often led by Riding Lights and supported by others in the church, to show that we were not desperately intense and pious, but knew how to laugh and enjoy ourselves in God's presence. This frequently relaxed the more nervous guests who were anxious lest they had come into a wild spiritual hothouse!

The Sunday services were always times of special joy. Adding 100 to 150 leaders, all hungry for spiritual renewal, to an already packed church, heightened the sense of anticipation considera-

bly. Both the family service in the morning and the evening service of Holy Communion were invariably times of unusual
blessing, and helped to put into some clear context the teaching
of the next few days' seminars. One couple expressed it this way,
and we had numerous similar letters from participants: "We
praise our living Lord that his Spirit was so powerfully evident in
the praise and worship, and in the overflowing love of the fellowship. Since coming home, we have wept together in the joy of the
Spirit, and for someone who like so many men is not given to
weeping, that can only be of God!" For most people, these
weeks were primarily times of personal renewal, which of course
is a necessary prelude to local church renewal; and often the
Spirit of God touched our visitors deeply through the worship of
his people. It was not uncommon to see individuals, including
strong, mature men, in tears. The services provided a visible
and tangible expression of much that we later talked about, and
as the week went on we touched on numerous additional aspects
of renewal and evangelism that were not immediately obvious in
the services.

From Monday to Thursday, we met together each morning
for worship and teaching, followed by a choice of seminars covering such subjects as ministry, healing, evangelism, small
groups, music, dance, drama, creative arts, youth work, counseling, children's work, catering. A team of helpers organized
lunches each day, and this was so carefully and beautifully done
that often it made an impression of its own, indicating that
renewal touched every area of our lives, not just our singing of
choruses! The bishop of Selby, Morris Maddocks, came to most
of the weeks and gave an excellent seminar on healing. This was
followed by the ministry of the laying on of hands, with the
elders assisting the bishop in this, and most of the guests coming
up for prayer. We became aware of the deep personal needs that
most Christian leaders have without a place to turn. Who can
minister to them in their churches? Where do they find the
counseling for themselves that they so frequently give to others?
For this reason the healing seminars, together with many other
opportunities for personal counseling, became a vital part of the

weeks. The presence of the bishop also helped the guests to see the approval of the wider church for these weeks, and indeed bishops from elsewhere even sent their clergy to us for renewal!

The strength and weakness of such a week lay in the fact that it was hosted by a local church, instead of the more usual set-up where a conference is organized by a specialized team of experts. This meant that the quality of teaching by seminar leaders was admittedly varied; but we felt that unless renewal could be seen to work within the context of an ordinary congregation—and we were a very ordinary congregation with a complete mix of social and educational backgrounds—it had nothing much to say to the church as a whole. Indeed, although the teaching and worship were generally appreciated by our visitors, it was the impact of the church as a living fellowship, with all its obvious faults and failings, that almost always made the most impact. One church leader who encouraged several other clergy to attend, wrote afterwards: "I have seen all the people who attended the recent Renewal Week.... They have all been blessed beyond words. One person put it beautifully, 'It was a glimpse of heaven.' This is precisely what our Lord means his living body to be." That, and countless similar letters gave us enormous encouragement.

From our perspective as elders we often seemed to be limping from one crisis in the church to another. "What next?" we often asked ourselves gloomily. We wondered if those who came to our church would have a glimpse of hell rather than one of heaven! But the gospel always speaks of God's grace in the midst of human weakness, sin, and frailty. There was no doubt about our weaknesses—one of our Renewal Weeks came immediately after the traumatic closing of the Mustard Seed—but somehow God's grace was still there among us, which is why those who came continued to be blessed.

The leader of one of the many Irish contingents who visited put it this way: "The value of a course like this lies chiefly in the encouragement and stimulus it gives. People coming from local situations which seem fairly hopeless can return home to weigh the biblical principles to see how they can be applied in their own churches. If God can do what he has manifestly done in such unpromising soil as the "redundant" churches in York, he can do new things in any place, if his people open up to him and in the power of the Holy Spirit respond where they are. This is the main message of the York weeks of local church renewal." Another said, "Here we felt God's love in action. He was really among us. We go back believing he goes with us."

For me, it was always a special privilege to pray with those who were longing for personal renewal. One older Norwegian pastor, who was also a gifted theologian, was so hungry to meet with God that he did not sleep at all the night before he came to York. I have hardly ever met a man who was so "hungry and thirsty for righteousness." Naturally God met him with unusual power. We did not say or do anything very much to him. God did his own work, and it was wonderful to see it happen. We never quite knew why those weeks proved to be such a turning point in the lives of so many who came, not least clergy and ministers, but that is what happened time and again. At a recent leaders' conference for renewal in Wales, seventy out of the eighty leaders present had been to our Renewal Weeks.

It is always important, however, to be sensitive to the momentum of the Spirit. When the wind of the Spirit seems to be blowing in a certain direction, we need the courage to hoist our sails and move as the Spirit leads us. But when the wind changes direction, we need equal courage to change with it. Recently we noticed a slackening of momentum in the Renewal Weeks, and I am glad to hear that the present leaders of St. Michael's have had the courage to stop them, at least for the time being. Perhaps these weeks will be started again at some later date, possibly in a different form. We need always to be open to the Spirit of God who is the Spirit of movement.

Constantly we need renewal. The Holy Spirit will never let us stay in one place for too long lest we become stale and stagnant. Always he is moving us on to make us fresh and relevant for the needs of people today. We can never cling to what is relevant only for the people of yesterday. If we do cling to those patterns we shall soon become spiritually sterile. "He who has an ear, let him hear what the Spirit says (*lit.* is saying) to the churches"

(Rev. 2:29). The greatest hindrance to the work of the Spirit is not tradition, since tradition can have a vital stabilizing effect in a confusing world of constant change. The greatest hindrance is *traditionalism,* or clinging to tradition for tradition's sake. The history of the church could be characterized first by the breath of the Spirit of God breathing new life into the church. Man then comes to regiment and institutionalize it, and the Spirit of God quietly withdraws. The institution, devoid of any real spiritual life, may then continue to rumble on unperturbed, sometimes for generations. Occasionally I come across certain church events which perhaps were highly relevant at one time, but over which we now see written the word ICHABOD—"the glory of the Lord has departed." This is when we need to cry out with the psalmist, "Wilt thou not revive us again, that thy people may rejoice in thee?" (Ps. 85:6).

18

Festivals for Reconciliation, Renewal, & Evangelism

"SOMEONE HAS TOLD US THAT A BOMB HAS BEEN PLANTED in the theater. Please get everyone out immediately!" I was leading the Merseyside Festival with a team I had taken with me from York. It was Youth Night, and the Empire Theater in Liverpool had at least two thousand young people in it. The program was to begin in ten minutes and then came this bomb scare. We asked everyone to leave as quickly and as quietly as possible, and within four minutes the theater was empty.

The police cordoned off the area while the theater was searched. Someone found a suspicious package near the electrical wiring system, so we were all ordered back to St. George's building at a safe distance away from the theater and the bomb-disposal unit from the army was called. There we were with two thousand young people standing on the steps of St. George's, looking like a typical football crowd. Then Alan Godson, an enterprising vicar in Liverpool and a great personal friend of mine, persuaded the fire department to erect some lighting, and the team did some drama interspersed with the singing of Christian songs and choruses by everyone. Alan guided a police van to where we were standing, and Bishop David Sheppard and I climbed in. Bishop David led in prayer, and I preached—all from the police van, using their loud speaker! It was the strangest pulpit I had ever used!

After well over an hour, the suspicious object was found to be only a hoax, and we went back into the theater to begin the Youth Night. Two thousand young people had gone out onto the streets, but the impromptu street theater had been so effective that 2,500 went back in for the main event. It was so extraordinarily successful that the following week, when we had another Youth Night, the theater was packed out with over 3,000 and more than 600 were turned away at the doors! Many young people found Christ on both those occasions, and we saw how marvelously God can turn any situation to his glory.

This was one of the many unusual incidents in the work I had started doing much of the time. Six years before in 1973, five respected Christian leaders had written to me over the course of a few months, and as far as I know they all wrote independently. However, each letter said roughly the same thing: "I wonder if God might be calling you to lead city-wide missions in the future?" For years I had been leading university missions, but this was quite different, and I tried to dismiss the idea. I knew that God had blessed the big events of the past, such as the Billy Graham Crusades at Harringay and Wembley in the mid-fifties. I felt sure, though, that such events were not for Great Britain in the seventies, even if they were still fruitful in other parts of the world. The whole pattern of evangelism had changed, I thought. In this day, "small is beautiful," as we had seen in small evangelistic home meetings. These cost nothing, required minimum organization, genuinely reached the outsider, and proved to be an environment where many were brought to Christ. I was not interested in any more big events.

Still, it was hard to ignore those five letters, especially when I received invitations to lead united church missions in Tonbridge, Bristol, and Sheffield in 1974–1975. I could not ignore the possibility that God *might* be saying something to me through all this, however unlikely it seemed to me at the time. I accepted the invitations and was pleasantly surprised when we had three thoroughly good missions. At Sheffield, for example, 13,000 people attended the meetings and at least 400 gave their lives to Christ. Furthermore, Christians came together from widely different traditions and denominations, and undoubtedly there was some spiritual renewal both in individuals and churches. We soon changed the name of these events from missions to festivals. I could see the value of the occasional celebration, especially with all the gloom, depression, and hostility of today's world.

It is commonly said that Christians need groups of three sizes for healthy growth into maturity; sociologists speak of this as a general need for everyone. The Christian ideally needs the cell, the congregation, and the celebration. The *cell* is the small house group in which there can be an intimate sharing of the faith. The *congregation* is what most Christians know about, the grouping when we come together each week for worship, teaching, and the sacraments. The *celebration* is the grouping when we occasionally come together in much greater numbers but still as members of one family in order to worship God, to proclaim the Good News of Jesus Christ, and to encourage one another in our faith. Even in secular terms we all benefit from celebration: birthday parties, weddings, anniversaries, and so forth. The Royal Wedding in 1981 of Prince Charles and Lady Diana was a time of rejoicing for the whole of England. Everyone felt better for it. We need these special events to lift us out of the drabness of much of our daily lives, and to remind us of some of the good and positive values in today's negative society. This is true also of the Christian family. It is easy to get engulfed by problems, personal or otherwise. But God's people are called to rejoice together in his presence, and to encourage others to do the same: "O magnify the Lord with me, and let us exalt his name together!" (Ps. 34:3). Festivals could never replace the mission and evangelism of the local church, yet if they are used to encourage local churches in their necessary and continuing work, they will be eminently worthwhile.

At Tonbridge, Bristol, and Sheffield I worked with the Fisherfolk. For several years I had been convinced of the value of setting the proclamation of the gospel firmly in the context of joyful worship. In this feelings generation I knew that most people need to feel God's presence and sense his reality before listening to his words. We found repeatedly in York that those who came to Christ in our services were initially aware of God's presence through the worship of his people. It was then my task as a preacher to say, in effect, "That which you have seen and heard I declare to you." This was the method of Jesus and the apostles when people realized that God was among them through healings or signs and wonders.

As much as I enjoyed working with the Fisherfolk, I looked forward to the time when I could travel with my own team. Slowly I built up a group of young people from St. Michael's who were gifted in music, dance, and drama—the drama section initially filled by those who later became Riding Lights.

Our first major commitment came in response to an invitation from the Bishop of Down and Dromore in Northern Ireland to lead a campaign for renewal in 1977. We went as a team of twelve and although inexperienced had a remarkably good time, especially during the closing five days in St. Anne's Cathedral, Belfast. One strict Calvinistic Presbyterian minister wrote to say "How my eyes were opened! What a new lease on life I am enjoying in Christ! It is almost like experiencing my rebirth once more. On the Sunday morning following your departure I felt I had to be man enough to stand and let my people know that God had blessed me at your services with a baptism of his Spirit. Many told me afterwards that I did not have to tell them because they could see the difference." Since then he has experienced deep fellowship with Roman Catholic priests who have themselves been renewed, something unthinkable previously. Another spoke of our time in Belfast as "the most spiritually rewarding experience I have ever known." All this was an important confirmation that God was with us in this new development, and we could see both clergy and laity come alive in the Spirit.

Once the basic vision of the work had been established and a regular fulltime team had come together, the invitations to lead festivals came in much faster than we could possibly manage. It soon became apparent that all these invitations needed careful researching. Which areas were ready for a festival? Were the Christians in that area beginning to work well together, especially the leaders? Did the proposed festival have the backing of the bishop and other denominational leaders? Was the Spirit causing a fresh hunger for God and a desire among Christians to make Christ known? Were we the right team for what was wanted? Obviously there are many different approaches, and ours may have been one valid way of communicating the gospel, but not the only one. It was clearly impossible for me to do the necessary research as the invitations grew in number. Providentially an elder in St. Michael's, Douglas Greenfield (who ran the Renewal Weeks), felt that God was calling him to help us in this, and, as consultant to an export pharmaceutical company he was given flexibility of time to combine his business with this research. Douglas over the years has proved indispensable, and without his careful investigation and practical planning we would have wasted many thousands of dollars and endless time and energy in fruitless work.

The simple plan has been for Douglas to follow up an invitation with a preliminary visit in order to discuss plans with church leaders. He would then submit a report, giving some indication as to whether a town or city was ready for a festival. If the report were favorable, we would arrange a 24-hour visit for the whole team, leading a festival of praise in the evening and holding seminars the next morning on evangelism, small groups, music in worship, dance in worship, and drama. By the end of that visit both the local church leaders and we as a team would have some idea whether a festival would be a good step in the future, and we would begin praying and planning accordingly.

The focal points of each festival have been evening celebrations each night of the week, marked by joyful, corporate worship and then preaching illustrated by drama or mime. These have always been festive occasions, even when we've taken very serious and challenging themes. The rest of the time has been filled with a wide variety of activities: visits to schools, universi-

ties, colleges, prisons, hospitals; lunches for businessmen; seminars for clergy; special meetings for ladies, the elderly, or the
sick; street theater in shopping centers; children's services;
workshops for local churches—anything relevant in the area.

Our overall aim has been threefold: reconciliation, renewal,
and evangelism. As far as *reconciliation* is concerned, it has been
thrilling seeing Christians of all traditions come together, usually
with very few exceptions in the city if any, and discover one
another in Christ. After an encouraging festival in Manchester
in 1978, one prominent leader in the city wrote: "I have now
been working in the city for over twenty-eight years and I can
honestly say that there has never been anything like it. . . One of
the outstanding features has been the way in which so many
churches have worked together (250 of them), plus the note of
celebration and just a real joy in the Lord himself." In Birmingham (1981) over 600 churches committed themselves to the
festival, and once again there had never been, in living memory
at least, such cooperation between the churches. We have always
felt that if new love and trust can be found within the body of
Christ in a given area, that alone makes the festival well worth
all the time, money, and effort involved. It is where "brothers
dwell together in unity" that the Lord "commands his blessing"
(Ps. 133).

Obviously the theme of reconciliation has been foremost in
our minds when leading festivals in Northern Ireland and South
Africa, and we have made it clear in all our meetings that all
people, no matter what tradition, race, or culture they belong
to, are welcome. Reconciliation, however, is never easy. In
Northern Ireland, for example, we have been openly opposed
by militant groups. In South Africa one attempted city-wide
festival was frankly a disaster. One of our biggest disappointments, however, was in Malta. In January 1978 Douglas and I
spent a week in Malta at the invitation of several leaders in the
Roman Catholic Church to see if we should lead a mission for
renewal in the Island for Roman Catholics. Douglas knew
Malta well through his business, and although I had an
extremely heavy cold throughout the week, I found it a fascinat-

ing time. We had many sensitive discussions and we knew that it was remarkable that we, an English Anglican team, should be invited for such a purpose. On the last day, when everything looked set, there was an objection from a totally unexpected non-Catholic source. We could do nothing but call the whole mission off, and all of us were extremely sad about it.

Our second main concern has been for *renewal*—encouraging fresh spiritual life both in the individual Christian and in the local church. The advantage of planning a special week, such as a festival, is that it gives everyone the motivation for doing what should be done in the normal course of the church's life. Christians come together to pray; they learn how to talk to their friends about Christ, and start doing it; they meet to study the faith, to worship, and to work on projects in the area, both evangelistic and social. In fact such good work has often taken place before our arrival in a town or city for the festival itself that I have frequently been told on the opening day, "If you had died before the festival had started, it would all have been worth it!" A curiously ambiguous remark—since I had not died, was it worth it after all?—but I know what I hope such a remark means, and I'm delighted that we have been the excuse for so many good Christian initiatives in different areas.

There can also be renewal in other ways. Many people have found renewal in worship: "For the first time in my life I am learning what it means to worship God," wrote one person after a festival. Others have discovered a new confidence in God, a new understanding of the faith, a new assurance of God's forgiveness and love. One of the most frequent and significant results has been the renewal of relationships. In the summer of 1978 we led a mission for the whole of Cornwall, based mainly in Truro Cathedral. The dean of the cathedral, who was nearing retirement, said that in all his long ministry he had never sensed such a powerful presence of the Spirit of God as during those ten days of the mission. One night I urged all those present who felt that they needed to put right some relationship to do so before they went to bed, if possible. "Talk when you get home," I urged. "Make a phone call; write a letter." Outside the big west doors of the cathedral were many telephone booths. I heard later that after the service there were lines of people waiting to make telephone calls, and I understand that many relationships were put right that evening. I did not know all this at the time. What I did know was that in the cathedral the next night the sense of God's presence was almost electric. The Spirit of God was no longer grieved through long-standing bad relationships and was thus free to move in unusual power. This is an experience known to Christians throughout the world in times of revival.

In Ipswich (1981) the hunger for God throughout the whole area was so great that we could not deal adequately with the crowds that came. The Corn Exchange building was booked for the main meetings, with overflows in the town hall nearby. On the opening night some 600 had to be turned away, many of them having come in bus parties from some distance. The next night an extra sound system was provided, and the meeting was broadcast to a crowd of 200 standing in the cold, dark streets, with cups of coffee and tea being taken to them. Eventually the Christians had to say to one another "Don't come unless you have to!" Not many churches say that today.

Following Ipswich we went to Northampton where we saw tremendous joy in God's presence as we came together from a variety of traditions. "The gift of joy has almost overwhelmed us" is how one Anglican leader expressed it. We also visited Wellingborough Borstal, the reformatory, when we were there. The prison chapel was packed with young lads, over fifty of whom committed their lives to Christ that morning. During the Leeds Festival (1977) we saw a particularly unusual healing. As the final hymn, "The Lord's My Shepherd," was being sung, a woman with multiple sclerosis realized that God was healing her. She got out of her wheelchair and, supported lightly by a member of my team, walked all around the town hall. In the course of a few months her healing became more complete, and she later married the bishop of the New Hebrides, now the bishop of Glasgow. These are only a few samples of the renewing work of the Spirit of God, and stories similar to these could be multiplied many times over.

My third and primary concern has always been *evangelism*. The reason why I have traveled with a team, gifted as they are in the performing arts, is that they are able to communicate the gospel much more effectively than I could with mere words. It was in 1977 that we first went to Crumlin Road Prison in Belfast and had two wonderful services for the prisoners, most of whom were terrorists. The chaplain said to us before we went in, "You will probably see more murderers in the next hour than in the rest of your life put together." We were decidedly nervous, but found that the combination of drama, music, and dance, and short, simple preaching created an instant rapport. When I led the prisoners in a prayer of commitment to Christ there was total prayerful silence. Many professed conversion that day, and the commander of one of the leading terrorist organizations wrote to tell me that he had been considering for some time becoming a Christian (an interesting point in itself!). "But," he went on, "after seeing your team I no longer had any doubts, and have now been saved by the blood of Christ." Later he told his prison chaplain, "For the first time in my life I feel free!"

I have many such letters from prisoners, including a number from terrorists, and most of those letters comment specifically about the vitality and communication of the team, and about the experience of feeling free once they had found Christ. In another prison in Canada, the prisoners wanted an encore, so we had to sing more songs, perform more sketches, and even preach more of the gospel. Once again many prisoners came to Christ in that prison, and as they were leaving one prisoner said, "You have brought us much joy in this prison today." Such remarks and letters are some of the most precious I have ever received.

I have found that the team is effective almost anywhere, especially with those who are just outside the church. In 1978 we held a festival called "Celebrate the Faith" in Newcastle-upon-Tyne. It was an exciting week and the crowded city hall was filled each night with a sense of joy in God's presence. The vicar and curate of an Anglican church in the city center had found it impossible to draw men to their church. It was a rough working-class area, with only a few elderly women attending the services.

But the festival gave the two clergymen an opportunity to invite lots of men they knew to the city hall. These men were thrilled with the sense of action, the drama, dancing, humor, and vitality. It seemed like the atmosphere of a football match, one of them reported. The result was that a number of those men gave their lives to Christ, and the whole work of that tough parish had a new lease on life.

We soon found that this threefold emphasis of reconciliation, renewal, and evangelism was at the top of most church leaders' agendas, and invitations to lead festivals became even more numerous. In 1980 alone, for example, I went (nearly always with the team) to Pasadena, Kansas, Vancouver, Calgary, Edmonton, Saskatoon, Winnipeg, Bedford, Rochdale, Poole, Chelsea, Cambridge, Wellington, Dunedin, Christchurch, Auckland, Brisbane, Launceston, Hobart, Melbourne, Sydney, Armidale, Tamworth, Canberra, and Sheffield. Almost all the places hold vivid memories for me, and everywhere we were aware of God's presence with us, both in times of blessing and in the moments of depression or exhaustion.

Increasingly it was obvious that God was using the team as a catalyst, something which is nothing much in itself, but either precipitates change or speeds up what is already taking place. There is very little that one team can do in a major city during one short week. But frequently God has used these festivals, superficial though they are in one sense, to stimulate his work that is already happening in that area. If we had not seen clear evidence for this, we would have stopped giving festivals very soon. The apparent glamor of jetting around the world disappears within a few days. It is not easy sitting in cold, drafty cathedrals, waiting for the stage or sound equipment to be erected before rehearsals can start. It is not easy traveling from one place to another so rapidly, so that it's difficult remembering which country you're in, let alone which town or city. It is not easy working in halls or churches where the facilities leave much to be desired. It is not easy living out of a suitcase for weeks on end. It is not easy sleeping, or trying to sleep, in strange beds for roughly half the nights of each year. My particular trial has always been damp beds. I have endured these so often that I now automatically carry with me a "survival kit for damp beds." If I suspect that the bed is damp, I put a mirror between the sheets. If the mirror mists up, I am left in no doubt! I then put on a black nylon raincoat over my pajamas, pull on thick socks, and climb carefully into bed. It is not the last word in comfort, but it's infinitely preferable to lying in a damp bed, getting chilled to the bone and sleeping little, if any. In one vicarage where the bed was damp—vicarages are nearly always the worst, and I usually stay in vicarages!—I wore my nylon raincoat as usual. Unfortunately, however, the vicar came in early in the morning with a cup of tea for me. I had to sit up in bed to drink the tea, and I think he was a bit surprised at my outfit!

Above all, it has not been easy having to say goodbye to my wife and children so often and being away for weeks on end. It has been more difficult for them. In order to give some stability for our children Anne has almost never traveled with me, and we have accepted the constant separations as necessary for the present time. We have worked hard to maintain communication however. Our schedule has been for Anne and me to write to each other usually every other day, and for me to write to Fiona and Guy twice a week. I have also telephoned every day when in this country, and once a week when overseas. We have also tried in various ways to encourage and support one another. Anne has helped, for example, by seeing to a lot of correspondence in my absence, making decisions where necessary and, with my secretary, trying to avoid having a mountain of demanding mail waiting for me on my return. Sometimes they have even hidden the mail from me until I partially recovered from a tour.

After the time when I spent ten grueling weeks in Australia and New Zealand, I resolved never to be away for more than five weeks at a time, but even so the work has placed strains on us as a family. In spite of this, however, God has been gracious, and our family life today is richer than it has ever been before.

I have had the privilege, of course, of traveling with a team, and the mutual support we receive from each other has been tremendous. All team members commit themselves for at least a year at a time, and I have always been glad when some choose to stay longer. With so many people who have been with me over the last eight years it is difficult mentioning any names in particular. All have played a special part in the work, and indeed in my own personal life. Most important, perhaps, is not the individual performance of gifted people, but the sense of Christ's presence through our oneness in him. The depth of we Christians' relationships in Christ always depends on the degree to which we are willing to share our lives openly with one another, and openness brings pain as well as joy. For example, sometimes I battle with depression. I never know all the reasons for this dark pit, as it seems to me. Some of it may be hurt pride. Sometimes it is obviously exhaustion—physical, mental, emotional, and spiritual. At times, when I am tired and strained, I get angry over an incident that may be quite trivial in itself, and then I get angry with myself for getting angry. As I suppress both forms of anger, depression is the result. Then I am even more difficult to live with than usual; I don't want people to get too near me, but I don't want them to go too far away either. My team members have always been extremely supportive when I have gone through these difficult times, and naturally others in the team have had their ups and downs as well. In this way, through our mutual caring for one another, the sense of our belonging together in Christ has increased.

At the end of the day we have found that we have nothing of ultimate importance to offer anyone, apart from Christ himself. If he can be manifested more clearly in our lives through our conscious weakness, we are content to remain weak and vulnerable. I have found both the traveling and the team work demanding in every way, but I am thankful to God for having drawn me into it against all my initial prejudices. I sometimes say that God sucked me in backwards into this work: I have neither wanted it, nor been ambitious for it. Fortunately God is able to use even reluctant servants to accomplish his sovereign will. And I have discovered, together with the team, a great sense of privilege and tremendous times of joy both in our fellowship with one another and in seeing God at work through us.

19

Facing the Future with a Festal Shout

ON JULY 26, 1982, WE CLOSED A MAJOR CHAPTER IN OUR LIVES and opened a blank page. After seventeen years in one house in York we moved to central London. The transition was not easy, and as I write this six months later we are still suffering profound bereavement. We knew that our relationships in York had been deep, but we had little idea how deep they were until they were severed. Next to literal bereavement within one's own family, this must surely be one of the most traumatic events possible. The sense of loss has been acute, and, as I have often counseled those who are bereaved, we have to let time do its own healing work. Certainly the Christians in London have not lacked kindness and generosity. Far from it. We know that we are a part of God's family wherever we go on the face of this earth, and the sensitive caring of many Christians here has encouraged us with God's love time and again. But deep relationships are forged through suffering and pain, as much as through joys and blessings. Without both warp and woof, no tapestry can be made.

"Joy and woe are woven fine" are the memorable words of

William Blake. Through a close friend in London God spoke to us saying that the riches we would find living here would be "the treasures of darkness." Richard Wurmbrand once said, "The most distant object you can see in the bright light of day is the sun. But in the dark of night you can see stars which are millions of times further away." We shall doubtless discover many of God's treasures through all our difficult experiences. Outwardly we have not been suffering at all, but the inward grief has taken us by surprise, and that is why I mention it. Many thousands of others must experience the same pain of parting, especially when their relationships have been bonded together by the super glue of God's love for many years.

"Why did you leave York at all?" is the question I am often asked, and it is not always easy giving the answer. I had always said that God called us to York in such a convincing way, despite all adverse circumstances, that it would require a spiritual bomb to get us out! It did not happen like that. Nor did we leave on account of the closing of the Mustard Seed or the split in the congregation. Indeed, while those problems were still around, nothing would have taken us from St. Michael's. It was only when the church had come together with a new unity and love, when the Holy Spirit was manifestly blessing God's work there again, that we could even contemplate the idea of departure.

The marriage ordinance in Genesis 2:24 is applicable: "Therefore a man leaves his father and his mother and cleaves to his wife, and they become one flesh." Leaving always comes before cleaving. Now that our spiritual children had grown up in maturity and were more than competent to take over the family business, it seemed that the time for leaving had come. No parents should hang around their children when they get married and start having a family of their own. Occasional visits are one thing; to live in the same house is quite another. We felt that the time had come for us as "parents" to give room for others to take over, without having us looking over their shoulders all the time to see how they were getting on. More than any other reason, it was for the future health and growth of the congregation at St.

Michael's that we knew, in our hearts, that we ought to move.

Besides all that, there were other considerations. More of my time was taken up with traveling, including many trips overseas, and London was an obvious center for this. I was receiving an increasing number of invitations to consult with church leaders, and nearly all of these took place in the metropolis. I also needed more time for writing and for preparing for the many speaking engagements I had throughout the year. As rector of St. Michael's I still had *some* parochial responsibilities, and crises were often awaiting me on my return from some overseas tour. Added to that, our children were at an age when a move was comparatively easy in terms of their education. If we did not move at this point, there would not have been a good time for them to do so during the next five years. Cautiously, we responded to a tentative suggestion from one or two leaders to base ourselves in central London.

It was not a sudden decision, and I have to remember that when agonizing doubts assail me as to whether we did the right thing. Over the course of nine months or more, we spent much time in prayer and asked the advice of several discerning Christian leaders, from the archbishop of York to friends in many different parts of the world. We kept hearing the same conclusion, "It makes sense." One or two prophetic words from those whose ministry I deeply respected confirmed that God wanted us to be available to minister for him in the wider church.

So we moved. Undoubtedly it was a step of faith. Although the bishops were behind the work we were doing, there was no ready-made job with salary and house for someone doing the work I am doing, and I have therefore become a "non-stipendiary clergyman." I have the further responsibility of paying and housing a team of about nine others. We have seen encouraging answers to prayer for God's provision. In York our team had been undergirded by a trust that had been formed through the generosity of one couple. After being renewed in the Spirit, this couple had given both money and property "for the advancement of the Christian religion by the proclamation of the gospel of Christ and the building up of his body the Church."

With our move to London, new trustees were appointed to manage what was to be known as The Belfrey Trust for our support. Even though we received a gift from the previous trust in York, our budget is more than four times as great as anything we have known in the past, and therefore, the same as many Christian organizations, we have to depend on the Lord month by month. Over the years I have never worried about money (perhaps partly because I have never understood it!) and I have always believed Hudson Taylor's principle that God's work done in God's way will never lack God's supplies. If in the future we ever find ourselves in financial difficulties, it will be a clear sign that we need to re-examine the whole work very carefully indeed. I have no desire to perpetuate beyond its usefulness what God seems to have raised up for the present time. He may well have quite different ideas in the future, although I expect we shall have some advance notice of this.

I sense that one reason for my being free from parochial responsibilities is that I can concentrate more on writing. I have never considered myself a writer, which is probably obvious by this stage, but through the encouragement of various people I have had several books published. Although I find the whole process nerve-racking, I have been amazed repeatedly by the way God has used these publications to touch the lives of individuals and churches. One woman wrote to me saying that after reading my book *How to Find God*, she knew that she must give her life to Christ. So she took a shower, dressed, did her hair, put on her make-up, and then knelt down by her bed to ask Christ into her life! She argued that if she had an audience with the queen, she would have done all that and more besides. So why not be presentable when meeting, for the first time, the King of kings and Lord of lords? It was fair logic, even though God would have received her just as she was because of her repentant and believing heart. I don't know if any of my other books has ever had such an unusual response; but I do know that through them God has touched the lives of many whom I shall never see this side of heaven.

One immediate joy in our move to London has been the creation of a new team. In York we had developed such close relationships in the various teams that I had been tempted to think it could never be the same again. For example, Phil and Joy Potter had been with me for four years and we had traveled around the world together, Phil ministering as a gifted singer and worship leader and Joy as a dancer and constant encourager. When they both left to go to Trinity College Bristol to train for ordination in the Church of England, they left an obvious gap which I knew would be hard to fill. It was not easy recruiting a new team, but we managed it, and in a remarkably short time we found that the Spirit of God was creating among us that same quality of shared relationships that I had known in the past.

We came together as comparative strangers at the end of August 1982, and our first festival was in Dartford two weeks later. The festival went wonderfully well and we were all encouraged. That was followed almost immediately by a five-week tour in Quebec and Ontario. Again I was excited not only by the specific contributions of the team but also by our fellowship in Christ. The new team has quickly learned how to care for one another, pray for one another, worship God together, and work well together. We know that the quality of what we do off the stage determines the value of our ministry on the stage.

Opportunities for Christian ministry abound on every side. We continue to receive more invitations than we can possibly accept, and we are currently investigating about thirty-five potential festivals both in this country and overseas. London itself is also a vast and endless mission field. Many clergymen and churches need encouragement and renewal. Other churches have the potential to send out lay teams, some of which could prepare the way for forthcoming festivals or work afterwards on follow-up. There is constant need for reconciliation, both within the church and within the wider circles of society. I continue to detect a growing hunger for God, and I know there is no possible unemployment within his kingdom. In the words of John Wesley, we need to keep "a cool head and a warm heart." The prospects for the future are like the beginnings of spring—bursting with potential for new life.

Our family has had encouragements as well since the move to London. We thank God for his provision of a house which has a considerable measure of privacy about it—something we find particularly helpful with all the demands of a public ministry. We've also had fun exploring all sorts of new places together, from Battersea Park where I enjoy rowing on the lake with Guy, to Wimbledon Common where Fiona rides and Anne exercises the dog.

We have found that life is full of changes, some joyful, some painful, and it is of inestimable comfort to know that God himself never changes. His steadfast love endures for ever and his mercies are new every morning. These are the rock-like certainties we must hold on to when everything else seems to be tumbling around our ears. We still have many unanswered questions. At present I do not know what my priorities should be, and where to give my limited time and energy. All of us as a family have found the move much more difficult than we had imagined, and at times it is easy for us to dwell on the negatives. However, what we do know, amid all our doubts and uncertainties, is that we cannot trust God too much.

Anne and I have seen that through the fires of past trials God has brought us into a much more complete marriage, and our family relationships are closer than they have ever been. We have seen how God can use even our sins and mistakes, when surrendered to him, to increase the beauty of his pattern in our lives, and to make us more useful in serving others. Nothing is outside his sovereign control and constant love. He is the One who turns our negatives into positives, especially in the darkroom of suffering. That is the confidence we always can have when we pray "Our Father, who art in heaven..."

Having written these words, I unexpectedly heard just yesterday that I have to go into the hospital in two days for a major abdominal operation which I'm told will knock me out of action for the best part of six months. Suddenly everything in the future has become uncertain, even life itself. I cannot say that I have no fears but I do know that "trusting God in every situation" is a reality for me and not mere words. Over the past few years I have been teaching large numbers of Christians all over the world the "festal shout," based on Psalm 89:15–17, "Blessed are the people who know the festal shout...For thou art the glory of their strength." Over the centuries God's people have often been exhorted to shout praises to God, and the great liturgies of the church have echoed these acclamations of faith such as "The Lord is here—his Spirit is with us" or "Christ has died, Christ has risen, Christ will come again." These glorious words should not be mumbled, but shouted out with ringing confidence since, if we genuinely believe them, they represent the greatest good news that we could ever know on this earth: whatever may happen, *the best is yet to be!*

One particular festal shout that I have taught, and which has rung through many cathedrals, city halls, theaters, and the outdoors, is a repeated acclamation in the Psalms: *The Lord Reigns!* When we gave this festal shout in Belfast Cathedral the day after a particularly horrifying bomb disaster in that city, we could almost visibly see the faith of the large congregation rise above their fears and sorrows. They were filled with a fresh confidence in the God who has in his hands the whole world, and therefore our own personal lives. That is the same festal shout with which I now encourage myself on the eve of my operation. I do not know what I shall experience, what the prognosis will be, or what changes will come in the future, but I can rest in the marvelous certainty that the Lord reigns.

Facing me, as I write this in my study, is a simple banner made by Janet Lunt who was once a member of our household and who started the banner group some years ago in York. The banner consists of words in the shape of a tulip: "TODAY my grace is sufficient for you." God calls us to live one day at a time, each day trusting in the sufficiency of the Father's love.

In York we often sang the following song, "For You Are My God," based on Psalm 16. It speaks for me completely now, since through the background of pain comes a ringing confidence in God himself:

For you are my God;
You alone are my joy;
Defend me, O Lord.

You give wonderful brethren to me,
the faithful who dwell in your land,
Those who choose alien gods
have chosen an alien band.

You show me the path for my life;
in your presence is fulness of joy.
To be at your right hand for ever
for me would be happiness always.

For you are my God;
You alone are my joy.
Defend me, O Lord. *